Surviving Catastrophic
Earth Changes

G. Cope Schellhorn

Books by G. Cope Schellhorn

*Extraterrestrials in Biblical Prophecy and
the New Age Great Experiment*

Discovering the Lost Pyramid

When Men Are Gods

Published by Horus House Press, Inc.

Surviving Catastrophic Earth Changes

G. Cope Schellhorn

 Horus House Press, Inc.
Madison, Wisconsin

Library of Congress Catalog Card Number: 94-75685
ISBN 1-881852-08-3

First printing May 1994

Published by
Horus House Press, Inc.
P.O. Box 55185
Madison, Wisconsin 53705

Cover art by Vicki Khuzami

Acknowledgments

The author wishes to thank Marie Dvorzak, Head, Geology-Geophysics Library, University of Wisconsin, for her kindly assistance and continuous generosity. Also thanks to Dennis Whelan, a true philologist, for his advice, encouragement and proofreading, and to Pedro Soto and CARE for sharing many of the earth-change photographs found in this work. And special thanks again to my wife, Patricia, for her timely suggestions and much work in producing a readable manuscript.

For Petoh and all others
who care so much about the future
of planet Earth and those
who abide there, if ever so briefly.

Contents

Introduction

The casual observer is already well aware that our world undergoes continual geologic changes and meteorologic shifts. The changes of the recent past, however--those that have helped shaped our parents' lives and our own--have not, with few exceptions, seemed acutely, much less chronically, life-threatening. Until, perhaps, now.

Within the past century geologists and other earth scientists have slipped into a dangerous pattern of spurious thinking. Specifically,they have insisted upon reflecting in their own theories and general attitudes a pattern they themselves have mentally created. They have then mistaken this mental creation for an actual reality. They have, in other words, been seeing what they expected to see, what they wanted to see.

This is not an unusual activity among human beings. Psychologists are quite familiar with it in all its guises. But it is especially dangerous when men of science indulge in it and tenaciously refuse to release themselves from it even when objective evidence indicates otherwise. The mental creation, the pattern, in question is best exemplified by the popular "uniformitarian" theory of geologic change. It carries with it a lot of satellite baggage. But briefly the theory goes like this: All geologic change happens very slowly; changes of the past were no different in kind or intensity than the changes we see occurring on earth today. While this is a relative statement, it is also an insidiously misleading one. Worse yet, this kind of thinking mistakes theory for reality and generalizing from insufficient evidence, and improper interpretation of evidence, for good thinking.

At this point, an analogy might be helpful. It isn't a perfect one but it is functional. What conclusions can we draw from the following situation? A man lives a quiet, unthreatened life for years, only to be run down and killed by a drunken motorist while he is still in the prime of life. Was it an accident? A statistical fluke, regrettable but predictable? What if we learn there are a great many drunken motorists on the road? If we ask the dead man (assuming he can speak) about his long, quiet life so rudely interrupted, we might get some interesting insights into the limitations of an exaggerated "uniformitarian" point of view. The skeptic will say I am confusing apples with oranges and trying to pass off a localized event as universal in its implications. Perhaps. But why, geologically speaking, do we find so many drunken motorists lurking in the earth's geologic history? And why are there now so many drunken motorist competing for our attention all over the world? Why are the numbers of these drunken motorists so rapidly increasing, and why are the "crimes" they commit increasingly violent? There is a crucial moment to be considered here in this particular case and also several crucial ideas that the analogy finally raises if we poke at it hard enough. If the dead man could speak, I have a feeling he would say the crucial moment was that split second of violence which tore his life asunder. The individual threatened by violent earth changes can readily sympathize with a situation becoming only too common today. We might conclude this story by suggesting that if we are to avoid being victimized by these increasingly frequent violent natural acts, we had better learn how to protect ourselves as best we can.

There are some geologists today who speak of "punctuated" uniformitarianism. They recognize that the "record of the rocks" indicates that earth's natural history has sometimes been sporadically violent, especially regionally. Unlike true traditional catastrophists, such as the British Deluvialists of the past century, they have a hard time dealing with such ideas as axis shifts, rotation cessations or pauses, extraterrestrial-object impacts, world deluges and much evidence of violent, cyclical changes. In fact many of them would like such ideas to go quietly away and quit disturbing their peace. They have no desire to shake the boat of contemporary orthodox consensus. Their predecessors, more by simple weight of numbers rather than by any convincing evidence (actually, the evidence is more convincing to the contrary), succeeded in overwhelming the position of the 18th and 19th century Deluvialists and other catastrophists. Lyellian geology (after Charles Lyell) triumphed and along with it a uniformitarian mindset. As with oversimplified Darwinism, Lyellian geology is a monument to how one man's musings, when taken to heart and worshipped, can become over time politically and academically correct ideology. Ideas to the contrary are akin to heresy.

Why do I offer this short history of the dirty underwear of geologic thinking? Mainly to highlight the present crucial moment, what is happening right now and what is likely to happen in the very near future. Also, I would like you to be aware of why orthodox geologists, and professionals of allied sciences, are not likely to recognize *that violent, massive earth changes have already begun today.* They will continue, most likely, to see what they want to see, what they expect to see because of their mindset. We, however, are now in the preliminary stages of even greater, more violent changes. The evidence continues to mount. What we are seeing is the prelude to the greater song, and a wild one at that. Unfortunately, except for the exceedingly wise, the greatly intuitive and the exceptionally acute observer of reality, the full weight of what is now commencing has not yet been recognized by the masses, nor is it understood by them, nor is it likely to be in the immediate future.

Scriptural prophecies, Judeo-Christian, Hindu, Amerindian, Mayan, Incan and otherwise, have spoken of these happenings. Many contemporary psychics and psychic channels have been registering these coming changes (e.g. Mary M. Wunder, Gordon-Michael Scallion, Jerry Wills, Edgar Cayce, Aaron Abrahamsen, Ruth Montgomery, Richard Kieninger, Paul Solomon, Ray Elkins, Lenora Huett, Baird Wallace, Beverly Jaegers, George King, Bella Karish, Clarisa Bernhardt, Doc Anderson, Rodolfo Benavides). A large number of contactees have returned from purported meetings with extraterrestrial visitors affirming that large-scale earth changes are imminent (e.g. Jerry Wills, Charles Silva, Eduard "Billy" Meier, Professor Hernandez (pseudonym), Sixto Jose Paz Wells, Antonio Nelson Tasca, Amaury Rivera, Joao Valerio, Hermines and Filiberto Cardenas). Then there are the prophecies of Nostradamus, who can hardly be called a contemporary but many of whose prophecies of natural calamities seem eerily directed towards our times. Of course, the established orthodox academics (and most academics are very orthodox) have laughed at such "evidence", while official government spokesmen make efforts to avoid pronouncements or acknowledge speculation except to admit that it is indeed a fact that large holes have opened in the earth's ozone layer, the planet's temperature may well be rising and, yes, California is due for a massive earthquake, or series of quakes, sometime soon.

Closed minds unfortunately beget closed minds. When one is blind and bull-headed, it is easy to step off the curb and get forcefully removed from this world by that "mythical", violent driver who awaits somewhere in time to make his violent unexpected appearance.

We don't have to believe the prophetic scriptures, the psychics and the contactees. Our own senses alone can lead us to a more accurate truth than we have become accustomed. It has become increasingly obvious day by day to careful nonscientific observers that the planet is more and more becoming roiled and wracked by destructive geologic and meteorologic processes. But if our lives are more in danger than they have previously been, it is logical to ask, What can we do? Where can we go? How will we survive?

It is questions like these that have compelled me to write this work. I was not planning to write it. I had talked about earth changes in several of my previous works (*Extraterrestrials in Biblical Prophecy and the New Age Great Experiment* and *When Men Are Gods*). Those works barely preceded the acceleration of earth changes that we are seeing today. In fact, in the first of those books I talked about "the lull before the storm." Since then the winds of change have literally picked up, the elements are now whipping more readily to fury. Because of this, I believe a practical work directed toward surviving the greater coming changes is merited, and I expect to see many more like it making their appearance in print in the near future. If the advice given here helps several people survive these coming changes, then the effort will have been well worth it. I will feel I have done my part in preparing our species for the worst and helping it survive and endure. If that sounds like false modesty, remember, it only takes one potent male and one fertile female working together to repopulate a world.

Exactly what kind of work do you have before you? First, it is not your ordinary survival manual. I do not believe stockpiling great gobs of ammunition and food alone is the ultimate answer to either physical or spiritual salvation. I have, as you will notice, concentrated in the early chapters on practical advice of the most basic kind, exploring such topics as safe areas, shelter, food and water supplies. These topics give rise to some considerations which are important, vital, if the potential survivor hopes to maintain his (her) body in effective operating condition. Such considerations, however, must be tempered by a mind and a spirit which are balanced and harmonious, otherwise all actions, no matter how assiduously taken, will sooner or later come to nothing. I suggest that no matter how intrigued the reader is with the nitty-gritty nuts and bolts of the earlier chapters, that he/she give as much or more attention to the later chapters. What good is saving the body at the sacrifice of the mind and spirit? There are, after all, worse things than losing our body. It is, at best, a useful container for gathering certain kinds of sensuous experience and is quite beautiful in its own right. There is no need to sacrifice it at this time if not necessary--unless all our options have been taken away. And if they have, well, that is fate, *que sera sera*, and we have no choice. Too often, however, history suggests that mankind mistakes ignorance and self-imposed reservations for destiny when a little more knowledge and a slightly greater willingness to flex the muscles and fire the mind might have caused personal and national histories to read quite differently.

This body we carry around, I am convinced, is only a meager part of man. We must remember that all bodies finally wither and die. Call it transmutation if you like. Spirits, however, endure. And no one is going to change cosmic law, alter cosmic necessity and write his own script no matter how willful or stubborn he is. He who thinks so is an egomaniac and a fool, and his *hubris*, his pride, is driving him to a fall the equal of MacBeth's (or Lady MacBeth's) in misery and as irreparable as Humpty Dumpty's.

I cannot guarantee you physical survival. No one can. All I can do is suggest that, if it is not your time to vacate this world, there are some actions you might take when you find yourself and those around you pressed by the exigencies of catastrophic earth changes. And God bless you, whatever your fate. I know you will survive one way or another. In body or out. Such is the law.

1

A Situation Assessment

Of primary importance to surviving violent earth changes is being in the right place at the right time. A person can plan carefully, take meticulous precautions about many things and find all of his or her efforts nullified by the simple fact that the chosen place of residence is in an area which cannot sustain human life during a period of natural calamities.

How inhabitable an area is will greatly depend upon what earth changes are happening at what time. As I write, millions of people have been made homeless in India by extraordinary monsoon rains, followed in late September by an earthquake (6.7 Richter scale) which, variously estimated, killed between 10,000 and 28,000 people. The Punjab breadbasket region of Pakistan and India has been severely damaged by high waters, especially this year's crops. The same rains and flooding have drastically affected parts of Nepal and Bangladesh. In fact, over half of Bangladesh was recently inundated. At the same time, in the United States the Mississippi river is raging. Thousands of Midwesterners in eight states have been made homeless. Concurrently, an earthquake registering 7.8 on the Richter scale has struck near the Japanese island of Okushiri killing scores, most of whom died from the accompanying tsunami which overwhelmed the island's shore shortly after the tremor.

In the last several years we have seen the Ring of Fire girdling the Pacific ocean become increasingly active. The eruption of Mount Pinatubo in the Philippines (1991-93) caused a significant amount of particulate matter to be hoisted into the earth's atmosphere, with a concomitant effect on world temperatures. The Mayon volcano, also in the Philippines, has erupted as well, although not with the fury of Pinatubo. There is some evidence that Popocatepetle, located in the Zona Volcanica near Mexico City and the fourth largest volcano in the world, may erupt soon. If it, and neighboring volcanoes, do erupt, they will in all likelihood destroy Mexico City and its environs.

A partial listing of some of the more dramatic (and deadly) earth changes that have taken place since 1989 is revealing:

Earthquakes

1990, May 30, N. Peru; fatalities 115
1990, June 21, N W Iran; fatalities 40,000+
1990, July 16, Luzon, Philippines; fatalities 1,621
1991, Feb. 1, Pakistan/Afganistan border; fatalities 1,200
1992, Mar. 13, 15, E. Turkey; fatalities 4,000

1992, Sept. 2, Nicaragua; fatalities 170+
1992, Oct. 12, Cairo, Egypt; fatalities 450
1992, Dec. 12, Flores, Indonesia; fatalities 2,500
1993, July 12, off Hokkaido, Japan; fatalities 200+
1993, Sept. 29, S. India, fatalities 30,000
1994, Jan. 17, Northridge/LA area (USA); fatalities 55+
1994, Feb. 16, Liwa, Indonesia; fatalities 100+
(note: increase in worldwide seismic activity over the
past 40 years)

Volcanism with Casualties

1991, June, Mount Unzen, Japan; fatalities 12+
1991, June, Mount Pinatubo, Philippines; fatalities
146+
1992, April, Cerro Negro, Nicaragua; casualties
1992, Feb., Mount Mayon, Philippines; fatalities 70+
(note: increase in activity of "Ring of Fire" and
worldwide volcanic activity over the past 5 years)

We need to be aware as well of such developments as
recorded flooding in North America, Europe and Asia in
the last several years; the continuing spread of drought
conditions in parts of Africa; record numbers of tornadoes
in the Middle West (1991); the increasing frequency of
deadly and destructive mudslides and forest fires
worldwide and the acceleration of "freak" weather
conditions such as the record low temperatures of the
winter of '94 in the Midwest and northeastern U.S.,
including unusual winter flooding in Ohio, Pennslyvania,
West Virginia and southern Europe.

This data, as I have indicated, is only part of the
evidence available that suggests major earth changes are

accelerating in intensity and relative frequency as the century progresses, and especially over the last several years.*

The times they are a-changing--obviously so. And first among these changes is worldwide weather patterns and the stability, or rather increasing instability, of the earth's crust in many places on the planet's surface. Yet if we are to believe the prophets, the psychics and the extraterrestrial contactees, it is likely that these violent outbursts of nature are only preliminary phenomena, a prelude in *staccato*, to a finale in *crescendo* of much more violent changes in the near future. If we have been observant, our senses have registered the uptick in the scale of change the past several years. If we have missed it, there is still time for most of us to apprise ourselves of the situation and take appropriate action.

It is rather useless, as I have already indicated, to expect much official confirmation that future changes may be even more destructive than those of the recent past. Governments are generally in the business of assuring their constituencies that all is well, not of increasing their anxiety level. They do not like to make predictions and run the risk of being contradicted. They fear public panic and widespread condemnation. God forbid that they

---

*There were, nevertheless, some particularly violent earth changes in the 80s, most notable among them the earthquakes which struck NW Algeria in 1980, killing 4,500 people, Southern Italy in 1980, killing 4,800, North Yemen in 1982, killing 2,800, Eastern Turkey in 1983, killing 1,300, Mexico City in 1985, killing 4,200+, NE Ecuador in 1987, killing more than 4,000 people, the India/Nepal border in 1988, causing over 1,000 fatalities, the China/Burma border in 1988, with fatalities in excess of 1,000, the great NW Armenia quake of 1988, with over 55,000 deaths, and the 1989 San Francisco Bay area tremor, which killed 62 people. Two volcanic eruptions, one in Columbia (Nevado del Ruiz, 1985) and one in NW Cameroon (1986), killed 22,000+ and 1700+ respectively.

should be blamed. The idea that anything at all could be beyond their control is anathema to them. Anything that would sour the sweetness of their patrons' sinecures is unsettling. The status quo of vested interests is to be maintained whenever and wherever possible by almost any means. Such is the tenor of big-time administration regardless of party affiliation. Those who have and control do not like upsets and surprises whether they come from people or nature. It was Alphonso the Wise (c. 1270) who said, "Had I been present at the Creation, I would have given some useful hints for the better ordering of the universe." Were he alive today, he would be the perfect official public relations man, the perfect spokesman for all governments which are smug in their belief that they can fix anything. If an agency such as FEMA (Federal Emergency Management Agency) had so much trouble responding to hurricane Andrew, which was after all, a localized disaster, what can we expect from it and other federal agencies when a rapid series of deadly, massive, natural calamities strike suddenly? Don't get your hopes up, they will probably be dashed into ten thousand pieces like carnival glass hitting the bricks.

So let's absolve official government here and now and not expect very much from it. We cannot after all blame it for most of the present and impending earth changes. These are, we strongly suspect, related more to natural, evolutionary changes of the earth and the solar system. Most are unavoidable, even if regrettable. Granted, atomic testing and the release of brom gasses (chlorofluorocarbons) have severely affected the ozone layer in the stratosphere and the ionosphere. The result of these releases has played a part in some of the meteorologic changes we are experiencing. There is little doubt about it. But we are going to be big-hearted. We don't hold grudges. We will for now forgive the industrialized nations for their carelessness, ignorance and sometimes willful stupidity. We have more serious things to think about. We have to consider how to save ourselves. And we have learned that holding grudges is a waste of precious time and destructive to the life of both body and soul.

It doesn't really matter, practically speaking, if the threat to do us in comes by way of an axis shift caused by the slippage of the Antarctic icecap into the ocean or by an axis shift whose impetus is the near passage of a large extraterrestrial object, such as the "dark star" mentioned in the Book of Revelation (Wormwood) and also by the Sumerians and Babylonians, called by them variously Nibiru ("the planet of the crossing") and Marduk.* A great worldwide natural calamity, either with an accompanying axis shift or without one, could also be caused by the impact of a large (two or more kilometers wide) meteor, asteroid or comet with planet Earth. A large object has been spotted, by the way, with infrared cameras and it may well be heading our way. Traditional ocular telescopes in the Southern Hemisphere have been trained in its direction. Is this the cosmic doomsday glob prophesied in Revelation to strike the earth *before* Wormwood makes its actual holocaustic appearance? Could it be Wormwood itself, or Nibiru/Marduk?

A contactee by the name of Amaury Rivera, who most likely is unaware of this telescope-search, has stated

---

*Both Zecharia Sitchin and myself have speculated on this Sumerian/Babylonian object. See Sitchin's *The Twelfth Planet* and my *Extraterrestrials in Biblical Prophecy and the New Age Great Experiment* and *When Men Are Gods*.

publicly that he was told by extraterrestrial visitors that a large object would soon impact earth not far off Puerto Rico with tragic results. Another contactee from Peru, Sixto Jose Paz Wells, has written, "The changes on the planet will obtain when this world enters a state of transition toward the fourth dimension, and the circumstance that hurries this change is possibly a comet or an asteroid striking the Earth." Still another contactee, Eduard "Billy" Meier, a Swiss farmer, has been warned about a "killer comet" (with an orbital period of approximately 275 years) that cyclically makes a passage close to earth causing havoc and severely affecting the planet's environment.

All this is food for thought, these statements both ancient and modern. It is the kind of fare, no doubt, that causes psychic indigestion. And yet it would, I think, be very unwise to totally ignore it or simply wish it away.

Very few people are aware that we barely missed being struck by a large asteroid twice within the last 4 years. By the same one. Its name is Toutatis, which means "protector of the tribe," an ironic name, it would seem, for such a pesky threat to civilization as we know it. It is one to two miles wide and was discovered in 1989 by a French astronomer as it made its first observed close miss of planet Earth. Toutatis has an orbit that crosses earth's orbit every four years. The proximity of its passages varies, but in 2004 it will pass within 1 million miles, which is considered quite close. "It would be catastrophic if it hit the Earth," said Don Yeomans, a research astronomer with the Jet Propulsion Laboratory. "It would throw up enough material to shut down the sunlight and the plants would have died. It wouldn't have wiped out everything, but millions and millions of people would expire."

Astronomers believe there are a lot more Toutatises out there, but few professional astronomers (except for Eugene Shoemaker and Eugene Levy) spend much time tracking them. Interestingly enough, most have passed by the earth *before* they have been spotted, a kind of after-the-fact observation that gives us absolutely no warning and, consequently, increases the danger quotient of being struck before we know what has hit us. Of course, as the wag might say, if it does you in, and you can't do anything about it, what's the difference?

Truth to tell, the world we know is exceedingly vulnerable to the kinds of catastrophes we have been discussing. It is little consolation that our conventional scientists, schooled in their own arcanum, assure us that an "extraterrestrial event," as they would call a sizable comet, meteor or asteroid impact, is likely to happen on average only every 250,000 (Wetherill, G. W.) or 5,000 (Clube, V.) years. The length of time depends to a great extent upon which scientist is offering a pronouncement. It is more than a little upsetting that their estimates vary so much and that they cannot come to greater agreement. Might this be an indiction that their speculations are, in most cases, only wild guesses masquerading as learned disquisitions. We can be forgiven, I think, for suspecting as much. And we can be certain that their failure to reach a narrower consensus, in other words, to agree on the odds of such occurrences, would be completely unacceptable behavior in Las Vegas.

There is a possibility that several of these calamities might happen at once or in short succession (a Book of Revelation scenario). Such seems to have been the case with the Great Deluge. Was this cataclysm only the main effect of other causes? And if so, what were these causes? Was the close passage of an extraterrestrial object one of them? Science today does not know. Indeed, many scientists give little credence to the idea of a Great Flood, despite all the evidence to the contrary.* They are nowadays quick to ignore the strong evidences of catastrophic events which were diligently ferreted out by early earth scientists such as William Buckland, William Whewell and Georges Cuvier, and all too willing to accept fragile evidence worked into tenuous theory, such as Louis Agassiz's glaciation hypothesis, to explain what others had better explained earlier. How much confidence can we have today in the establishment, party-line utterances of geologists and geophysicists about preHolocene geology when we realize that "our" understanding of the earth's more recent history (Holocene, or the last 10,000 years) is so poor? Where are the maverick, honest voices who are willing to go against the grain, even risk their academic appointments and their grants in the name of a more accurate truth? Have all been so utterly brainwashed, their nature as real men and women so reduced? In an age where the spirit of true science, honest science, is supposed to be dominant, have we become a race of moral pygmies? We will never learn all there is to learn about earth history or ourselves until we cast off all pre-conceptions, no matter whether they are our own in the first place or someone else's that we were bid to accept.

---

*See Immanuel Velikovsky's *Ages in Chaos, Earth in Upheaval*; also the works of George McCready Price, Joseph Prestwich, Henry Howorth and other like minds for evidence of a Great Deluge.

2

Searching Out Safe Areas

Where then can we go when the elements are raging?
Where hide until the worst is passed? What part of
Mother Earth will offer us shelter, a safe haven?

These questions pose a large problem which quickly
humbles the seeker after an answer, even a partial one.
And rightly so. There has been much vanity expended by
many well-meaning people, and probably some very self-
deluded ones, who revel in the idea of offering advice.
Too much of this advice is voiced as if it came directly out
of the mouth of the Great Nazarene or God Itself. You are
welcome to it, should in fact consider it, but I would not
stake my life too much on most of it. I cannot help but
recall what Daniel was told (and what the Great Nazarene
said) about the timing of such apocalyptic events. The
prophet was instructed to 'seal up' his 'latter end' visions.
'Go your way, Daniel, for the words are shut up and

sealed until the time of the end.'

Are these the 'times of the end'? Many think so. On July 11, 1991 a full eclipse of the sun took place in Mexico City and elsewhere on the North American continent. Seventeen different Mexican citizens at various locations around the city videotaped the appearance of a bright UFO during and after the height of the eclipse. Many Mexican interpreters believe this congruence of events may not have been coincidental but may well fulfill ancient Mayan prophecy which, according to the Dresden Codex, foretold an eclipse of the sun before the 6th Mayan age. At that time, the Codex relates, great earth changes would commence and the Lords of the Sky would make their reappearance.

Are these interpreters on the right track? I would be inclined to agree, with one reservation. I am very fallible and have been wrong many times before. Maybe I am wrong now. We shall see. As the saying goes, time will tell us. If this is, indeed, the climax of apocalyptic times, of the beginning of the Mayan 6th age, we won't have long to wait.

There is another recent indication that an old age is being ushered out to make way for a new one. The Hopi Indians of the southwestern United States have many prophecies which pertain to this kind of change. Some mention earth changes, to be sure. But one I find particularly interesting. It has been said that before the Hopi's great prophet, Massau, returns from the East bearing sacred tablets, two of his messengers would appear to them, one carrying a sun disk, symbol of the cosmic breath, the life force, the other bearing a swastika, the true Aryan symbol, reflecting the motion of all life everywhere.

These two symbols were presented to Thomas Banyacya at high noon on September 28th, 1993. Thomas Banyacya is a member of the Coyote Clan. His function is chief interpreter to the traditional Hopi elders.

It is dangerous to presume one has the dispensation to prophesy accurately in the name of the Creator, even if these are "end times." I prefer to believe the Nazarene when he says, speaking to his disciples in reference to the exact timing of apocalyptic events, 'But of that day and hour no one knows, not even the angels of heaven, nor the Son, but the Father only.' I think it important to be aware, whether you believe in extraterrestrial visitors to the planet or not, that the word "angel" in English comes from the Greek word *angelos,* which means "messenger," and it is this Greek word that translators chose when they were searching for the closest approximation in meaning to the original Aramaic word. I believe it is also important to realize that, almost without exception, UFO visitors to the planet have refused to set dates to the violent earth changes that they have directly and indirectly alluded to on a number of occasions. They have, however, implied repeatedly that these changes are either imminent or to be expected in the not too distant future.

With all the above cautions having been iterated, with you now having been duly warned about grasping too eagerly at the coattails of the first would-be prophet who offers advice about safe areas of the world and this continent during catastrophic earth changes, I offer you several speculations from individuals whose "visions" seem in my eyes to be more compelling than do those of their many competitors. This is, admittedly by its nature, a subjective enterprise. I make no promises, offer no guarantees. There is no way of knowing whether these various visions are gospel truth or miss the mark completely until the events either happen or do not happen. By then it will be too late to offer a final appraisal. But I do, nevertheless, find the following material interesting enough, and thought provoking enough, to pass it on.

Hugh Auchincloss Brown's *Cataclysms of the Earth* has been out of print for many years. The work deserves a better fate because Brown is one of the early, and more convincing, advocates of cyclical axis shifts. These shifts, he maintains, occur roughly every 7,000 years and are caused by either the arctic or antarctic icecaps becoming too large which, sooner or later, causes the globe to "tip" on average 80 degrees from its former position. These days we would call that tipping an axis shift. It is a phenomenon which in the past was hotly disputed among scientists. More recently, however, with the accumulation of better evidence, orthodox science has been willing to recognize that such shifts probably have occurred in the earth's ancient past, although few are willing to argue that such a shift has occurred within the last 100,000 years.

During what he calls Epoch No. 1, *which preceded the latest shift of the globe,* the Mississippi river flowed west to east and the climate was tropical. The Sudan Basin, now found in Africa, was then at the North Pole. In Epoch No. 2, the Mississippi flowed southward and the Hudson Bay Basin was at the North Pole. During summertime the upper reaches of the river were fed by melting glaciers.

Hugh Auchincloss Brown traces these shifts through 11 epochs. Suffice it to say that the kinds of evidence he offers for periodic "careenings" of the planet are fascinating and deserve more attention. What is most interesting about his work, and most pertinent to the focus of our inquiry, is his warning about the present epoch. He believes our time is running out, that the icecap at the South Pole has grown dangerously large, and if we do not figure out how to control its growth, how to remove or divert some of its buildup, sending it perhaps into the warmer oceans of the world where warm waters can lave it and melt it away, we are doomed. If this is not done, if we do not succeed in controlling it, planetary human life as we know it is finished. The icecap will slip, the axis, because of displaced weight, will shift and we will have most catastrophically ushered in a New World under a New Heaven. If there are perchance survivors, the night sky will indeed seem different and "new," because of the axial realignment. This is not exactly the happy New World or New Age envisioned by many Christians and New-Agers. It is, more accurately, a repetitive horror show where momentary viewers become the ultimate victims.

Hugh Auchincloss Brown does not go into great detail about possible safe areas during one of his "careens" of the globe other than to say he believes those residing on the equator and at the North and South poles would fare best. Obviously, in this day and age the percent of the world's population now found in any of these areas is miniscule compared to the world's present total population.

A second visionary who has had a large influence on present earth-change thinking is the famed "sleeping prophet," Edgar Cayce, of Virginia Beach, Virginia. During his lifetime Cayce gave over 14,000 readings, of which approximately 9000 were medical diagnoses and of which only 15 predicted geologic events for the period 1958-2000. These particular events foretold disaster, catastrophic turmoil culminating in an axis shift sometime between 1998-2000. Because of the high accuracy level of his medical diagnoses and other predictions, many people believe that there is a large possibility that Cayce's earth-change predictions have great innate credibility until proven otherwise.

What exactly did Cayce say in those 15 readings? The main issues stand out like red flags:

(1) Very destructive earthquakes will destroy Los Angeles and San Francisco.

(2) New York City will be destroyed after catastrophic West Coast quakes. The northeastern coastline, including the Connecticut coastline, will be submerged.

(3) Much of the southeastern coastline, including the coasts of Georgia, South Carolina and possibly North Carolina, will be submerged.

(4) Ultimately, the western coast of North America will be submerged for hundreds of miles inland. Omaha, Nebraska, will become a port city.

(5) Much of the Middle West will also be submerged except for parts of Illinois, Ohio, Indiana and much of southern and eastern Canada. Virginia Beach, Virginia, will become a seaport.

(6) The Great Lakes will finally empty into the Gulf of Mexico.

(7) Northern Europe will be changed "in the twinkling of an eye" as much of it becomes inundated.

(8) Most of Japan will be destroyed and submerged.

(9) New land masses will appear in the Atlantic and Pacific oceans. Parts of ancient Atlantis will reemerge from the depths of the sea.

(10) All of South America will be "shaken from the uppermost portion to the end."

(11)   Catastrophic disturbances will shake both the Arctic and Antarctic as well as the South Pacific.

(12) Between 1998-2000 the axis of the earth will shift causing many of the worst changes.

Cayce's scenario for our time is greatly worrisome if it is even half-accurate. If it is close to being thoroughly true, it is doubtful that the greater portion of mankind will survive. Appraising the earth-change utterances that had issued from his own mouth, Cayce drew an obvious conclusion in a reading given on August 13, 1941: "No wonder, then, that the entity feels the need, the necessity for a change of central location . . . The choice should be made by the entity itself as to location, and especially as to the active work . . . ."

But how does an "entity" make that choice? Where is safety to be found?   How can one be sure he(she) is choosing a safe area? And just how safe is safe?

These questions have an urgency and an inevitability about them that do not go away. They must be faced and answered by anyone who has concluded, for whatever reasons, that large-scale earth changes are imminent and who wishes to make an all-out effort to preserve themselves, spirit, mind *and body*.

Before we address these nagging questions head-on, it might do well to consider the writings of Dolores Cannon who has recently released the third volume of her Nostradamus series called *Conversations with Nostradamus: His Prophecies Explained*. The series is a unique one, purporting to be actual conversations with the famous seer who is speaking to us from *his time* to *our time* to, as Cannon puts it, "warn us about *where* and *how* we must concentrate our energies during the next several years in order to curtail some of the more disastrous events in our future which he has foreseen."

Cannon's material is not directly channeled by herself but was taken from hypnotized subjects between 1986 and 1989. She explains that Nostradamus believed in the theory of 'probable futures,' that is, multiple possibilities, and this reminds us of the Seth material of Jane Roberts. "He believed," says Cannon, "that if man had the knowledge, he could see which time line his future was headed down and reverse it before it was too late." Such an idea is not, per se, illogical and does not contradict mathematical probability theory. Indeed, some theorists have argued that the idea makes theoretical good sense. I personally find such theorizing fascinating and intellectually attractive. Whether you have much confidence in this type of material or not, I think you will find Cannon's maps of post earth-change geography, which I have reproduced here, particularly interesting. You might want to compare them with Cayce's thoughts.

One of the first things about the Cannon/Nostradamus maps which strikes the eye is that they do not fundamentally contradict the Cayce material. In fact, they are much more detailed than anything Cayce foretold. Cannon's subjects verify, it would seem, Cayce's suggestion that a large segment of the Middle West would remain above water (but an even larger portion of Cayce's continental U.S. is submerged). Parts of Iowa, Kansas, Nebraska, Oklahoma, Arkansas, Tennessee, Kentucky and North and South Dakota remain elevated above sea level. Also, confirming the predictions of a good many other psychics, a portion of the Southwest and Rocky Mountain states remain elevated. The west coast of California, not surprisingly, has returned to the deep.

What if Cayce's and Cannon's material turns out to be

relatively accurate? Does this mean a human being can save himself(herself) by relocating immediately to Missouri or Arizona or northwestern New Mexico? Perhaps. And perhaps not. It would be presumptuous and probably foolish to assume that these states (and others like them), even if they survive and remain elevated, will remain totally unscathed. They most likely will be deeply affected and troubled by what is happening near them and elsewhere in the world. They may, for instance, be subjected to tremors in the earth's crust, though possibly not nearly to the extent of the neighboring land masses. Missouri, after all, contains the New Madrid fault which produced the most intense earthquakes that America has experienced in historic times, even seismically greater than the one which levelled San Francisco in 1906.

If an axis shift does occur in the near future, at least several effects are predictable. It will cause the oceans as they now exist to send their waters journeying in huge walls of water which will wash, actually overwhelm, a good portion of the earth's dry land. A shift of axis will most likely also cause a shift of the world's tectonic plates. Some land masses will rise almost instantly, perhaps to thousands of feet skyward as may well have happened to the land upon which the city of Machu Picchu, Peru, was built in the distant past. Other land areas are likely to be percipitously plunged under new oceans. Tectonic shifts of the earth's plates can be counted on to trigger volcanism. New volcanoes will arise, old ones become active again. We can expect, in such a situation, many of the now quiescent volcanoes in the Pacific Ring of Fire and elsewhere in the world to burst open anew almost in unison, spewing forth particulate matter and acrid gases (some of them deadly) by the millions, billions of tons.

Climates will be instantly altered, as happened, it would seem, in what is now Arctic areas where the quick-frozen carcasses of mammoths are still found to this day with remnants of buttercups and other temperate-zone vegetation lodged in their stomachs. Whether the air will be breathable, and whether there will be enough sunlight for things to grow, is doubtful. Most animal life, and a large percentage of our flora, will shortly succumb.

Can human beings survive this kind of alteration? Even if they find themselves standing on *terra firma* after the worst of the worldwide flooding and landmass repositionings? Some, perhaps. The lucky, the extremely hardy and those who have, to a degree, prepared themselves and are willing to "tough it out." If you feel intuitively you are one of these, or wish to be one of these, read on. It is not necessary to completely despair.

As far as we know, at least a remnant of humanity has always survived even the worst of earth changes in the prehistoric past. These are the legendary Noahs, Deucalions, Ziusudras, Utnapishtums, Fohuts and others celebrated by various cultures. And we have proof that some of these legends are true. We're here, after all, alive today because some of our ancestors did not give up but managed somehow to endure and even reproduce themselves. There is something deep in the innermost nature of man, it would see, that insists, if at all possible, on surviving even the worst calamities, the most challenging circumstances, to live on and prevail that its progeny might better flourish in a kinder age. Call it mindless persistence or brutish tenaciousness. Call it pure animal stubbornness or simply the "will to live," if no other words come to mind. I have a feeling, however, that this kind of survival has less to do with luck and a lot more to do with certain qualities of the spirit and mind than we most often suspect. Whatever we call it, we should always remember that we would not be here today if *it* had not been strong in our human (and hominid) ancestors. We should be thankful for that. How much dumb luck had to do with the survival of any remnant of humanity at any given time is impossible to say. But to count on simple luck in the near future to carry us through a new series of earth changes would probably not be very wise and very likely could be fatal.

Who can we rely upon to give us final counsel other than ourselves? Who knows us better? If we are not capable of an Emersonian-type of self-reliance when put to the test, if we cannot trust ourselves, we are in grave trouble. But self-reliance as popularly understood today is a far cry from the American pioneer spirit and the ideas of Ralph Waldo Emerson, Henry David Thoreau and like-thinking mortals. Today's ideas of independence and self-sufficiency are something altogether different. They make up a far too ego-centered, materialistic credo to sustain us during the kinds of trials that severe earth changes will bring (have already started to bring) us.

The kind of self-reliance I am talking about is based on the harmonious functioning of the total man. And by "total man" I mean a being whose body, mind and spirit are all fully operational, each responding to its respective role, playing its ordained part, but each aware in its own way that it is a cooperative part of a greater functioning whole, and aware that the totality is lessened, reduced in significance and performance, if that totality does not strive consciously and unconsciously to be everything it can be. I am speaking particularly about an interblending of being that is responsive to, and feels intimately connected with, all being, all things of heaven and earth. This "total man" ideally has no hang-ups, no vendettas to settle with anyone or anything, no time for *angst*, for modern versions of neurasthenia, nor for misplaced existential ideas of hostile or indifferent environments. He(she) seeks peace, equilibrium and harmony generally while there is a specific, lasting yearning for experience and new knowledge. But at times he(she) recognizes we are all corpuscles of the same Great Body, acknowledges our peculiar and fascinating matter and energy configuration which makes us uniquely ourselves, while at the same time, and paradoxically, also makes us an indivisible, living, breathing creation. A *corpus infinitum*.

As has been obvious, modern society does not support this kind of living--or these kinds of ideas. Finding a truly "total man" has become a difficult proposition. Total men are almost as rare as condors or bison. Yet each of us must strive to be one, especially if we wish to have much hope of successfully surviving great earth changes. The more "total man" we can become, the easier our transition will be to the rough conditions we should expect after massive geologic rearrangements.

The total man is not afraid of his spiritual nature, neither is he self-conscious about making use of it. If by prayer or intuition he can find what he believes to be a safe area, he probably had best yield to this inner counseling. The more mentally inclined person may wish to use his everyday reason to deduce that there are some areas of the world which are less prone to seismic activity, have fewer fault lines, are higher in present elevation, have less or no present volcanism and, therefore, are, hopefully, safer, more desirable areas of habitation. Whatever the case, once a move in residence is made and the individual sets his mind to remaining there, the die has been cast. He(she) must live or die by the choice, come hell or high water or flaming brickbats from the sky.

In other words, each of us must finally make our own decisions and live by them. We may counsel with the Creator, friends, Ouija boards, the *I Ching*, rune stones, psychics, loved ones or relatives but the final choice of where to locate or relocate is ours. We are all finally personally responsible for our own destiny, which once upon a time was a truism that seemed patently obvious to most people and was taken for granted. In the present age, it is becoming much rarer to find those who are willing, much less want, to take responsibility for their lives.

This failure to take personal responsibility seriously is often accompanied by the adoption of a fanciful and bogus definition of freedom with a peculiar Orwellian twist: we find virtual slavery masquerading as freedom. In addition we often overlook how closely related personal responsibility is to true freedom. This, however, is no new phenomenon to the 20th century, although the willingness to adopt popular false images as a definition of self seems to be increasing as the century nears its end. Psychoanalyst Eric Fromm made the observation several decades ago that most individuals seem to prefer the illusion of freedom to the real thing. The real thing, of course, carries a heavy cargo of responsibility which most would prefer to jettison or have someone else service for them. Fromm noted that one of "the principle social avenues of escape (from the exercise of personal freedom) in our time" is " the *compulsive conforming* as is prevalent in our democracy."

Of course, there are no guarantees that if you exercise

your innate gift of personal freedom to make an earth-change decision, you will necessarily make the right one. Any individual choice may turn out to be a poor one. Some areas of the country which seem so promising and such logical choices today, such as parts of the Central U.S. which are being much touted by certain speakers and writers, may turn out to be anything but life-sustaining. Possibly the number of humans who survive this accelerating series of earth changes will be miniscule, as I have already suggested elsewhere. It is true that our best efforts to survive physically may ultimately be meager and of little practical account. Fate may hang heavy with us, depriving us of our bodies. But never let anyone tell you that it is not important to make the effort to survive. Whether you win or lose your body is not important in the grander scheme of things. What is important, however, as the popular saying goes, is how you play the game, important to you personally and important cosmically. The latter idea may flabbergast the jaded materialist or the fatalistic mind. So be it, if so. I am only too willing to elaborate, to reduce, if nothing else, the shock value to the disbelieving of being told that, yes, even the smallest cosmic atom, including the hairs of one's head, are duly accounted for and valued equally by the Creation. And I am willing to maintain the position outside of a Christian framework, if you wish me to do so. The proposition does not fundamentally depend on Christian arguments, although it does not intrinsically contradict them either. But woe finally to the being who believes he is only flesh and bone. For him the death of the body is the end of all seasons, the loss of all hope.

Life is precious, in body and out. All life. Everywhere. If you believe that, you probably also believe, as I do, that it is important to try to sustain it wherever it is found, even here in this tired, old, earthly body, unless there are some exceptionally cogent reasons to the contrary, and I cannot think of any.

There is no doubt much experience to be gained from this complex, and demanding, earth life. It is not an oversimplification to say that we are here to learn, to increase our spiritual and mental understanding of a world such as this one. We can be pretty sure that there is no other world exactly like this one. And we can assume, I think, we are not here by accident. It is questionable whether there really is such a thing as cosmic accidents, which does not, however, rule out the possibility of free will. Whatever the case, we have been given a dandy chance to learn the upper and lower limits, the joys and despair, of the physical human body and the material world which surrounds it.

Our experiences, we discover, help us to better understand others as well as ourselves. We become at once more graceful social beings (kinder and gentler) and more complete, rounded, singular selves. There is no contradiction here. Each type of learning facilitates the other. After our sojourn in this world, we take what we have learned along with us, like a shopper who has been to market. Some learn a little more, some a little less, but we are all better for the interaction. Stasis is an illusion. The cosmos continues to move, to transmute itself and we along with it. To resist is futile, impossible. Even the idea of regression may be an illusion, a misapprehension of what direction is and is not. Not only should we, with our limited perspective and understanding, refrain from judging absolutely our neighbor's character, we should withhold drawing final conclusions about the course of his life. It may, after all, be headed where it must go or should go for reasons that are beyond our knowing.

Sometimes in the midst of turmoil, when our personal lives seem momentarily askew, or when as now the Four Horsemen of the Apocalypse are grimly riding forth, we tend to doubt the value of the experiences we are having. But just as life is precious wherever found, so are the singular experiences that go along with it. It is the movement of the life force in the cosmos which is creating those experiences. (Everything moves all the time.) We must build on them, somewhat like coral building an atoll: each experience like a small separate organism; all experiences *in toto* making up the larger reef, the complete personality. Each organism or experience by itself doesn't seem like much. Over time, taken together, they build a mighty aggregate. That aggregate is supremely and uniquely us. There is no other like it in the universe. No two alike anywhere. Each has its own supernal beauty. Each its singularity--as does everything which makes up the conglomerate of Creation. Each reflects the ineffable course of cosmic life that we study so hard to understand.

It would seem inadvisable to cut short the course of a human life in this world, even if it should momentarily seem unreasonably harsh, as if nature would rise up to confound us and then crush us in our confusion. The temptation to give up hope is exceedingly great during times of violent earth changes. It is natural enough, part of the great swing and play of human emotions, one side of the great yin-yang field of opposites upon which the cosmic game takes place--but we must not yield to it. We must have or develop the fortitude, which comes from an act of will, to withstand all assaults. And we must make a conscious choice to do this. Yang, the active principle, must, in this case, dominate yin.

If we have unconsciously chosen, as I believe we have, to live this particular life, then to give up in midcourse is to deny ourselves some of the potential fruits of our labor. We must make the unconscious now conscious. We must choose willingly, purposefully, with eyes wide open. If we are put to the test, then let us be tested.

As human beings we can only do our best, and there is some nobility in that. If we do succumb, we do so with the knowledge that we hold life dear and did all we could to maintain it even in the most adverse circumstances. If we lose the struggle to save our bodies (our "containers"), so be it. We have after all gained greatly in experience, pushed ourselves quite likely to limits we never thought possible, learned to do things we had previously thought impossible, and yielded finally, grudgingly, with our last breath, to overwhelming odds. We will have made, then, the transposition from this world to another honorably, not with a bang but surely not with a whimper. It can never be said of us that life passed us by or caught us comatose or acting like catatonics. We went looking for it and its myriad possibilities. We yielded to our fate *but not before our time and with our self-respect intact.*

And besides, with such an attitude, some of us will most likely survive, guardians of the race's seed, to become new pioneers in a New World under a new sun. That is the legacy of spirit which those of us who pass on can leave with pride to those who succeed us.

You can be sure the great multitude of men and women of our time will not concern themselves with such thoughts, not anyway until the day the earth changes begin with force to touch their own lives. They will be busy marrying, partying, working and doing those accustomed things which mark the pattern of their lives. Do not expect them to worry themselves much until the coming cataclysms overwhelm them. And then expect them to be much astir amid great confusion and mayhem. Those who read the early signs of vast change will be thought foolish and branded as alarmists and fatalists. It serves no purpose to try to proselytize. Those who wish to know the truth will find it. That is the way it has always been and will probably always be. Those who are observant will see it and hear it and otherwise sense it as it begins to manifest itself.

Those who have no interest in reading the signs are best left alone. The old adage about leading a horse to water is appropriate here. You cannot, nor can I, make someone drink from a cup they refuse to acknowledge.

Neither should you, nor I, try to instill a stronger will to live in someone who does not wish to. Each of us is personally responsible for discovering the preciousness of life, including his own. Those who adamantly refuse this responsibility may have to lose their present life to discover the preciousness of it. And this includes the learning-value of it. It is not an easy thing to watch those we love fail to recognize this preciousness. Some seem hellbent on wasting life or abusing it. But mere words from us will probably not change their thinking. They must be allowed to go their own way peacefully amid the turmoil around them, whether this turmoil is self-created or proceeds from the unfolding of natural events. They must be allowed to find their own way even if their effort, or lack of it, costs them their physical life, which it well may. These are harsh lessons. But this is no time for us to play God. At this point, we must maintain our humility and realize we cannot teach those who do not wish to be taught. They must instruct themselves, and we must be gracious enough and wise enough not to interfere.

There is an old Chinese proverb that says, "He who would know himself should sit. He who would teach himself should walk." Every man must do his own sitting and walk his own mile.

3

Finding Adaquate Shelter

There exists a vast underground shelter in West Virginia attached to the White Sulphur Springs Hotel. It was constructed for U.S. senators, representatives and other high government officials to use in times of national calamity such as nuclear attack or massive, catastrophic earth changes. It is a pity that officialdom didn't think of you and me when they planned this resort with its elaborate underground bunkers. But bureaucrats are notorious for thinking of themselves first and we should not be very surprised at being overlooked and underappreciated. I can well imagine a world in which only bureaucrats survive. It is a desolating thought, worse perhaps than fallout and tsunami combined. Thank you, brothers and sisters, for thinking of us but I am going ahead with my own planning, and if my neighbors and I by some good fortune do happen to survive, we will consider having a true democratic plebiscite and reconsider the appropriateness of appointments and special privileges.

White Sulphur Springs is not the only insulated spot. The Strategic Air Command (SAC) has mammoth underground facilities near Colorado Springs, Colorado, and there are numerous subterranean military bases in the West and Southwest such as near Dulce, New Mexico and Groom Lake, Nevada.

Most of us do not live by large natural caves or cavern complexes or impressive artificial excavations such as the Swiss government has constructed for its citizens. It is doubtful our government will ever open wide for any reason the thresholds of what underground installations it has. And even if it were willing, the number of people these excavations could harbor is relatively small in comparison to the potential number who might be seeking shelter.

Where, then, does one shelter oneself? What kind of shelter might be available? What kind might a man or woman (or several people working together) construct quickly to protect themselves until, at any rate, the worst, most violent, earth changes have passed?

These are large, haunting questions, and there are no easy answers. What qualified answers that can be offered will not satisfy some people. But when there are no other alternatives, they will have to suffice.

Let's start, then, with the most obvious temporary solution. The average basement, unless it has been specially constructed, will only do for the most temporary residence. Why? Because it is too exposed, too vulnerable. The ceiling above, like the rest of the upper structure, is probably flammable and not strong enough or durable enough to withstand the punishment of extremely high winds. And by high winds I am talking about velocities of several hundred miles per hour or greater in the event of an axis shift or impact by a sizable extraterrestrial object..

What kind of structure can withstand such winds? First choice would be small caves or larger caverns. We are back to where we began, so it would seem. Several decades ago it was said that the Third World War would be waged with nuclear weapons and the Fourth World War would be, most likely, contested with sticks and stones. The assumption was that nuclear war could easily set us back culturally to the Stone Age (and still potentially can, complete with a lethal, radioactive atmosphere and "nuclear winter," as postulated originally by scientists Turco, Toon, Ackerman, Pollack and Sagan). So could, of course, devastating earth changes either in concert with nuclear war (as described, for instance, in the Book of Revelation) or all by their catastrophic selves.

Living temporarily in a cave, however, does not necessarily mean that all earthly civilization, and the culture that goes with it, would be absolutely lost. Caves have their advantages. They can withstand the impact of nuclear blasts if the blasts are at a distance. What is more, they can absorb the thrusts of high winds--even winds in the 200 to 300 miles per hour range or more which we have already associated with an axis shift. The temperature in large caves usually hovers around 50 degrees in temperate latitudes. And the entrances of most caves are rather small and can usually be made smaller with some effort. Why such a necessity? First, to block the passage of acrid and poisonous gases. (More about gases and the need for protective measures later. See chapter six, "Maintaining Breathable Air.") Secondly, a small opening makes this new abode less conspicuous to marauding strangers.

The trouble is most people do not have a cave or cavern nearby. If you are one of the fortunate who has one, then by all means make use of it. Outfit it for such emergencies. Spend as much time and money as you can reasonably afford to make it as safe and comfortable as possible.

What is the next best alternative after a cave? Probably an underground shelter constructed with your own hands--or the hands of hired professionals if you can afford to hire out the job.

There are several ways of preceding, some more economical than others. I built one myself for several hundred dollars out of used cement blocks. This was a structure 14 feet long and 10 feet wide with 6 x 6 white oak timbers, stacked side by side, for a roof. Atop this structure I dumped three feet of topsoil.

But let's start at the beginning. After I found a load of used cement blocks that set me back half of what new ones would have cost, I hired a bobcat operator to dig out an excavation in the side of one of my hills. (It isn't hard to find a hill on my land in southwestern Wisconsin because I have very little flat ground on my 14.6 acres.) I chose a spot close to the house. Thus I was able to justify my project to my wondering neighbors as a convenient root cellar. I knew it would serve as a fallout shelter should the leaders of the world finally go irreparably berserk and, what was primarily on my mind, as a small, protected home for my wife and I in case of severe earth changes.

I instructed the bobcat operator to level an excavated

area 16 feel long and 14 feel wide. This allowed me room to work--to pour a concrete footing 12 inches wide and 12 inches deep around the base. It would be upon this footing that I would lay my rows of cement blocks until they reached approximately 8 feet tall. I mixed my footing concrete by hand in a large wheelbarrow. The same wheelbarrow worked fine for the mortar mix I needed to cement the blocks together.

At the front of my blockhouse I left an opening 7 feet high and 36 inches wide so that later I could build a door frame and attach a good, sturdy door. I got lucky and found a used metal door at a junk shop which worked just fine. The day I hung that door I complimented myself on my good fortune, patted myself on the back, which is a good thing to do once in awhile when the days are hot and the work is hard. But I am ahead of my story. Door hanging comes late in the process and is kind of a capstone ritual, a celebration of rites of passage. There is much to do, however, that precedes that act, some of it time-consuming and demanding but all of it instructive.

Projecting outward from each side of the front door I built a retaining wall, also out of cement blocks, and I stepped these downward gradually until the walls were each one block high. This allowed me to pile up soil against these walls on each side, thus further insulating the structure and keeping the wind away from the entrance.

I left a flue opening approximately one block square in the rear wall 4 feet from the floor. This allows me to use a small wood stove as a heating unit. For the main stovepipe projecting upward about 6 feet above the topsoil at the rear of my root cellar--fallout shelter--earth-change hideaway, I used a piece of strong 12 inch drainage pipe (galvanized culvert pipe). Actually, I used regular 6 inch stovepipe inside the shelter itself and ran it from the stove part way up into the culvert pipe. This seems a practical, durable solution to heating in general and the rust problem of regular stovepipe. The piece of new culvert cost me about $30.00 and was well worth it, although a used piece of culvert pipe in good condition might be purchased for almost nothing.

I have run clay drainage pipe through each side wall of the shelter and outward from it for a distance of about 4 feet. The reason for this is to assure myself of a source of fresh air. If conditions warrant, I can partially plug these outlets with cotton or fiberglass insulation, thus filtering out airborne particulate matter completely and acrid gases, such as sulfurous gases, at least partially. It concerns me greatly that if very many volcanoes erupt on earth simultaneously, the atmosphere will not only be heavy in particulate matter, which can be quite smothering, but most likely poisonous to breathe. I will talk more about what can be done to protect oneself from these gases later.

After my efforts, I stepped back to survey the results of my project. Completion of the whole affair had taken no more than two weeks of intermittent labor and, as I have said, several hundred dollars. The sweat-labor I gladly supplied myself. If I had contracted for poured concrete walls, which is an option, the cost would have been much greater. If, by the way, you decide to choose this option, make sure you specify reinforced walls at least 8 inches thick.

In earthquake prone areas, which mine is not, cinder block walls may collapse. I would then advise constructing the shelter-bunker out of heavy timber or poured concrete. It isn't at all impossible to mix and pour the concrete yourself, although we are talking about a more complicated procedure. If you opt for this alternative, I suggest renting a mixer with a small electric motor. And keep mixing and pouring until you have the whole job completed. If you pour wet concrete over concrete that has already set, the bind is inferior and you have a weaker wall. Try to keep pourings homogeneous and of one piece.

Anyway, I finished my shelter and it was both a source of mystery and delight to me. I would sneak out of the house from time to time and walk the short distance to my covered blockhouse--to stare and wonder at the product of my labor. To say I wasn't immensely pleased would be lying. I had, I believe, that grin around my lips and dimpling my cheeks which I have noticed my black cat, Jujubee, sporting after he has impaled a particularly obese field mouse and made short-order cuisine of it. If someone had surprised me in those moments, I think I would have jumped involuntarily and made a grand fuss to cover my embarrassment.

Never, so far, have I been disappointed. I believe my shelter to be serviceable and reasonably comfortable. It is true that poured concrete would have been somewhat stronger and more earthquake resistant. But all in all, I think what I have will do well for my needs.

It is wise to keep in mind that, no matter what you use for construction material, when an earthquake begins, it is imperative to get out in the open, away from tall trees and all structures which might topple. After the last tremors, you may return to your blockhouse to check for damage. Resume residence if, and only if, it is safely intact.

I realize many people do not have enough room to build such a structure. If a person has a yard, he or she may justify building such a structure in the name of a root cellar. I would not necessarily tell my neighbors that I suspect severe earth changes are going to soon reduce the neighborhood to rubble. No purpose served by that. Besides, it may give them an excuse to make you the local "character" in town. If they insist on knowing why you want a root cellar in this day and age, tell them you prefer your vegetables and fruits fresh and do a lot of canning. At the worst, they will probably think your enterprise quaint and you a bit old-fashioned. You may be called a food faddist behind your back. But what do you care? Just hope they don't ask to see all those processed jars of nature's bounty that you are supposed to have produced. Learning to can and preserve fruits and vegetables in other ways is, by the way, a very wise thing to do for those who seriously hope to increase their odds of survival.

Some people say, "Why go to all the bother? Our governments, federal, state and local, will make, I'm sure, every effort to help us. They will supply us with shelter, food, water . . ." As I have said several times already, don't bet your life on it. Severe earth changes will cause mass confusion. Shelter, food and water will be at a premium. When the effects of the changes become overwhelming, government relief efforts will most likely collapse, cease to exist or exist in such a disorganized, limited, rudimentary form that they will be of little use. It is best to be partially prepared for the worst all of the time. And, if you're extra cautious, to be as fully prepared as possible all the time. It is preferable in the long run to be considered a little strange by the neighborhood, and survive, rather than to be one of the politically correct Joneses, who don't make it. And, if it's any consolation to your ego, you probably won't be considered strange at all by other survivors. You may find yourself being held up for emulation as an exceedingly prudent, extraordinarily wise example.

4

Emergency Food and Water

It is a disturbing fact that most city dwellers and suburbanites have little idea of how to feed themselves or find adequate potable water during times of an extended emergency. What is to be done, for instance, when the supermarkets are closed or empty or destroyed? When the water mains are broken or polluted? It is a sad commentary on the preparedness of Western life in general and American life in particular that so few people have any experience in raising an adequate supply of vegetables, grains and fruits, keeping husbandry or creating healthy, drinkable water. The day of the Victory Garden, which fed so many Americans during the Second World War, is long past and at best a dim memory. Many who learned or honed their gardening skills then have died and their skills and know-how have passed on with them.

He who cannot feed himself is truly a hostage to Dame Fortune. And she is not always a friendly lady. Your life and mine ultimately depend as much on adequate sustenance as they do on any other single thing. And our bodies well know it. All we have to do is go twelve hours or so without food and water and our bodies, habitual creatures that they are, begin to remonstrate and rebel.

It is not only the city dweller and suburbanite who have forgotten, or never learned, how to grow foodstuffs effectively. Even some farmers now seem strangely vulnerable--a colossal irony in what is the world's greatest food-producing nation. How could such a thing happen? Rather easily. Most farmers today are highly specialized. They raise only one or two crops--say, corn or soy beans or wheat only, or just beef. Many farm families have quit gardening. The frontier kitchen garden is now, if not a rarity, at least not a predictable appendage of farm living. Most farmers, whether male or female, do not grow their own vegetables, fruits and grains any more. They, like their city cousins, buy them at the local supermarket. That makes them, like city dwellers, all that much more vulnerable in times of great natural crises.

Many farm wives have forgotten the tricks of successful gardening so well known to their mothers and grandmothers. Women traditionally were the keepers of the kitchen garden, as is still the custom with my Amish and Mennonite neighbors. Women supplied the fresh produce, did much of the milking, tended the chickens, collected the eggs. The men were more involved with hog, beef and grain production, mending machinery and raising new structures. There tended to be men's work and women's work, a highly stratified lifestyle that, for better or worse, recent consciousness-raising attempts have done much to undermine.

Several years ago, during the '91-'92 recession, I watched and listened to a short, poignant news story. The attending correspondent, mike thrust forward, was interviewing a middle-aged Iowa farm wife. Bad times had obviously come to this family. There wasn't enough money being generated by their operation to float the mortgage and the bankers had foreclosed. The woman, standing on the gravel driveway with the wind whipping her hair, had this to say, "We have no food to eat. We're going hungry. My husband is driving 180 miles a day round trip to a second job."

With these words the cameraman panned the wide expanse of the large dairy farm. Here was acre upon acre of rich, good land. But there was no garden in sight. Why hadn't these people planted a large garden? I wondered. Its only cost was a few dollars in seed and some wholesome exercise. There just didn't seem much common sense involved here. The truth is most farmers, like medical doctors and academicians, have become overspecialized. And when the right hand has forgotten what the left hand can do, has even forgotten that there is a left hand much less what feats two healthy hands working together can accomplish, then the "body"--and the mind and spirit as well--is in trouble. Then farmers can starve, even under a full sun with plentiful rain. Even when the elements are not conspiring to wreck havoc.

You won't hear of Amish and Mennonites starving today. First of all, they would not allow neighbors to succumb to such a plight. Secondly, they don't overspecialize their operations. They raise a little of this, a little of that. They know better than to put all of their eggs in the same basket, as the old commonplace saying so wisely warns.

Before I talk more about kitchen gardens, and also about gathering and hunting, a word or two about *emergency rations* seems appropriate. Ads continually appear in "survivalist" magazines and other publications offering a large line of canned and dehydrated foods, certifiably vacuum packed, complete with can opener or pull-tabs. Canned distilled water is also available upon demand. The potential consumer should be aware, however, that all of this is very expensive stuff. The price tag for several months worth can easily reach $700 to $1,000 or more, depending upon the size of your appetite and the weight of your purse.

There is, luckily, a more common sense approach. It is heavy in staples, cheap and nutritious, if not the most varied diet known to man. The foodstuffs of which I speak are easily obtainable. You can collect them yourself and store them with relative ease. Here's how to do it.

Go to a discount grocer or wholesale grocery warehouse and buy several one-hundred-pound bags of dried beans and rice. Do not buy polished rice because the exterior shell or husk of each rice kernel contains much of the rice's nutrients. Buy brown rice or unpolished rice. Also buy a case or two of salt and as much sugar as you wish. Both of these latter items do not cost very much, and you will probably be pleasantly surprised how little beans and rice cost when bought in volume.

Now lug your booty home. Put the dried beans in one-gallon or larger glass or plastic jars. Do likewise with the rice. Place a piece of Saran wrap over the mouth of each jar, then screw on the lid. The Saran wrap helps create an airtight container whose contents will keep almost indefinitely. Now place these vessels in a dry, cool, dark storage area to await the day they are needed. You might check the beans and rice every six months to make sure no vermin are present. Chances are, you will find these dried rations doing nicely in their static environment.

Salt can be used as seasoning or preservative. Sugar, besides being a sweetener, is a source of quick energy. It is also a preservative of sorts.

Another relatively inexpensive and nutritious staple you might consider buying in quantity is oats. "Mares eat oats and does eat oats . . ." and so can you, lots of oats, if the circumstances demand it. If you've already been trained on oatmeal from childhood, you have a head start. Buy generic oatmeal and save money. One hundred pounds will last a long time. Take your oats home and store them as you did the dried beans and rice.

Two to three hundred pounds of beans, rice and oats should supply a couple of people nourishment for several hundred days. Granted this is not *haute cuisine*. It is not fancy fare but a sturdy, basic ration that is intended to save your life and tide you over until you can develop a source of permanent, alternative food. These alternative foods will not be brought to you and laid in your lap. The National Guard, Red Cross or Salvation Army will probably be nowhere in sight. They will not be knocking at your door with armloads of victuals and jugs of pure water. Most likely your "alternative food sources" will be those you create from your own garden or from gathering and hunting, by using your hands and through the sweat of your brow. I will elaborate much more on these sources, and ways to expedite their development, in chapters nine and ten. But for now, let us consider the one *sine qua non* none of us can live without--fresh, pure water.

We take fresh, clean water for granted in the United States. There is not, for instance, one city in Mexico where the drinking water at this moment is truly safe (although Cancun and Puerto Vallarta make the claim), and this state of affairs is true of most of the rest of the world. You might say that too many of us are used to taking too much for granted and that we have over time become spoiled in our expectations. Some extended travel aboard, however, where conditions of sanitation are much inferior to North America, is a revealing, sobering lesson in greater reality.

Even now parts of the United States are beginning to suffer from a lack of fresh water for agriculture. California and Texas are sterling examples. During periodic droughts which deplete the reservoir system, California does not have enough fresh water available to satisfy the demands of urban businesses and residences and still meet, at the same time, agriculture's ever rising need for more. Deep-well pumping has so depleted the local aquifers in some parts of Texas that many small towns truck in their drinking water supplies. The once picturesque Rio Grande river, which separates Mexico and Texas, is now a polluted mudhole because so much of the river's waters has been diverted upstream for irrigation and damaged downstream by indiscriminate dumping. According to U.S. Geologic Survey data, many of the states west of the Mississippi will soon face a great fresh water crisis. One can only marvel at human nature which has sent so many people scampering westward and southwestward like so many lemmings to an environment which cannot support them. Factor into this equation massive earth changes and we have all the makings of an assured disaster the limits of which appall the mind. After earth changes, it is not difficult to see that precious little, if any, safe water would be available for survivors.

In fact, with massive earth changes, *no water anywhere can be assumed safe to drink.* What can we do about this probability? First, we can use the time-honored method of destroying bacteria and waterborne viruses. We can boil the water we plan to drink 15 to 20 minutes. Bring the water to a thorough, fast boil. Then let it cool. Unwanted sediments will settle slowly to the bottom of the holding vessel, especially if a day or two is allowed to pass before the water is carefully switched from the holding vessel to the storage container. If possible make sure the storage container is as airtight as possible. No sense in contaminating clean water with new airborne particles and fresh bacteria and viruses.

The wise survivalist with some foresight will have purchased inexpensive plastic containers, such as the 5 gallon water jugs used by serious campers, and stored water for an emergency. This water should be checked from time to time to make sure it is still "sweet," just as all sorted foodstuffs should be checked for staleness, infestations of vermin and rancidness. If problems have occurred, or you have some doubts, refill containers and put them away until the next spot-check or until needed.

The serious backwoods camper and hiker often carries Halizone tablets. These can be purchased from any camping supply dealer at little cost. However, be warned. Halizone tablets are not completely dependable. They have their limitations and deteriorate with age.

A better, more dependable source of water purification is iodine. Iodine kits can be purchased from many pharmacists at reasonable cost, and they are good insurance. A kit consists of a one-ounce transparent glass bottle with a tight cap and about 5 grams of USP-grade resublimated iodine crystals. These crystals are reusable, up to a thousand times.

There are also water filtration devices on the market which will decontaminate impure water and even remove the iodine taste from treated water. These pieces of equipment, however, can get expensive. If you don't mind a slight taste of iodine, then resublimated iodine crystals are the economical way to go. To be extra careful, boil water first, then treat with iodine crystals. Better an extra step for safety than typhoid, dysentery or cholera, all of which can be fatal.

There is another way to obtain emergency fresh water of which few people are aware. This involves constructing--more properly, digging--a solar still. The still is a simple device and can be made as follows:

Dig a hole about 2 feet deep and approximately 3 feet across. Choose a low, sunny spot for best results. Place a small pail or container, which can hold up to 2 quarts of water, in the bottom of the hole. Run a thin rubber or plastic tube from the bottom of the pail to slightly above surface level. Then cut a 6-foot piece of clear plastic (3 mil in thickness will do fine, 4 mil and above is better) into an oval shape, place over hole and weigh down the edges of the plastic sheet with stones. Make edges airtight by sealing them with soil. Now place a stone in the center of the plastic sheet. This stone should be heavy enough to depress the plastic sheet, allowing condensed water to run down the inside of it and drip into the pail. Do not use a stone that is too heavy, forcing the sheet to break or collapse. *Also, make sure the plastic sheet does not touch the pail.* Usually water will begin to collect in about an hour, and one quart or more a day is not too much to be expected. Up to 3 or more quarts of drinkable, distilled water can be obtained per day from such an apparatus if slightly impure water is added to the bottom of the hole in the beginning. This impure water will distill into drinkable water over time. Even small quantities of vegetation can be placed in the bottom of the hole. Sunlight will draw out the water from this vegetation as it slowly desiccates it. This water will also condense onto the plastic sheet and finally drip into the pail.

Now, as water collects in the pail, all that is left for you to do is draw it out through the surface-level end of the aforementioned plastic (or rubber) tube. Use the tube as you would use a straw. This exercise is not as thrilling, perhaps, as sipping a milkshake but is, in times of real need, a much more fundamental activity. There are times, I think most people would agree, when nothing tastes better than pure water; there have been times when kingdoms would have been traded for a taste of it.

The solar still can be used anywhere, in the desert, on the plains, in mountainous terrain. The only condition which can totally inactivate it is a complete lack of sunshine over an extended period of time. This would effectively short-circuit the condensation process. Let us hope we do not have to face such a contingency in a time of need. If conditions warrant, boiling or crystal treatment or a combination of both must be the alternatives of choice. Next to light, it is water that is the true staff of physical life. Without it there can be no bread--and no survival.

5

Basic Impedimenta: Clothing, Tools, Pots and Pans . . .

What does the well-dressed survivalist wear? A cynic with a sense of humor might answer, Whatever he can. Certainly, whatever is practical and available should be put to use, Mr. Blackwell notwithstanding. Nevertheless, a little sartorial planning will go a long way toward insuring survival and at least a minimal comfort level.

It is you who have a lot to say about what is available. And it is you who must decide what might be, under various climatic possibilities, practical gear.

It is not, rest assured, necessary to spend great amounts of money on survivalist clothing. We are not outfitting ourselves for a safari or a 19th century grand tour of the continent. Neither are we practicing simulated war games. We are not trying to impress anyone, even ourselves. L.L. Bean and Abercrombie do not count for much here. What you need, you may already possess or you may find it quickly at K Mart or Wal-Mart at a reasonable price. So much for *haute couture*. High water and high winds have a wonderful ability to take the hot air out of high pretensions.

Most of us have clothing stuck away in our closets and bureau drawers that is suitable for average, everyday wear. Many of us are not, however, prepared for temperatures below zero, *especially if we have to live out-of-doors for an extended period of time in such weather.*

Some of the summer togs already in our possession will probably do for roughing it in warm weather. Some will not. Trouble is too much of what we have is short-sleeved, short-legged and flimsy. We need relatively thick cottons and khakis to withstand abuse.

Why should we worry about the sun's rays? What if there is a further erosion of the ozone layer? What then?

Both cosmic rays and ultraviolet light cause skin cancer, including melanoma. A cavalier attitude about direct sunlight, which is now prevalent among many people, especially the young, is a ticket to a dangerous lottery. And the name of the lottery is Grief. Therefore, even the present earth changes (and the erosion of the ozone layer definitely qualifies) argue strongly for possessing, and using, several warm-weather outfits that have long sleeves and cover the full leg.

We cannot say just how much the sun's penetration of our ionosphere, stratosphere and lower atmosphere will be affected by massive earth changes. If we use the evidence of foraminifera die-offs, for example, that mark so many of the major geologic time-boundaries (including the Cretaceous-Tertiary, Eocene-Oligocene and Frasnian-Famennian), we can   probably speculate with a fair probability of being accurate that these die-offs were caused partly by an alteration in the quantity of sunlight reaching the earth and its oceans. And what caused this diminution of light? Perhaps asteroid or comet impacts in the cases of the three boundary examples given above. At each of these boundaries, traces of the isotope iridium are present. (See Richard Muller's *Nemesis*.) These traces do not appear immediately above or below the boundary levels and, because iridium is a predictable byproduct of an extraterrestrial impact, we can conclude with almost complete certainty that impacts in the past have happened and, with some certainly, that they have appreciably altered the life cycle of this planet. On a more immediate note, we can conclude that the changes underway because of ozone depletion will be significant for all living flora and fauna. If we lose too much ozone, if cosmic radiation increases greatly, we, those of us who are left, may well find ourselves driven underground to survive. We are not now troglodytes but we may, out of necessity, find ourselves subterranean.

Extreme cold may also be the trigger which drives us underground. If we do not own a good parka with a warm hood, we should seriously consider purchasing one. As well as warm, lined gloves. And a pair of subzero, heavy-duty, winter boots. And a face mask, balaclava-style or otherwise, is also recommended. All of this winter apparel can be purchased for less than $200 at a discount store. Not much of an outlay, really, considering the insurance value.

A sudden axis shift could drop temperatures well below zero in a few minutes of time. This drop might be accompanied by winds of several hundred miles per hour. It is hard, and frightening, to imagine what kind of windchill factor such conditions might create. But unfortunately there is a precedent. We have the perfectly frozen mammoths of northern Siberia. Several complete specimens have been found, the first along the Lena river in 1806. The partial remains of thousands of mammoth carcasses have been found in the far northern Russian islands, many still frozen and edible. Mammoth tusks have been traded in the area for centuries. What is most outstanding about these finds is not there sheer numbers, which are staggering, not that some are found, surprisingly, in a standing position frozen in a mixture of ice and debris, but the fact that the mammoths often appear to have been caught off guard and quick-frozen to the spot, their stomachs filled with temperate-zone vegetation (partially digested and undigested). What great earth change happened so fast it turned these woolly denizens into frozen statuary? Did an axis shift accompany it? Cause it? Was it, as others including myself have suggested, the same great catastrophe which we have traditionally called the Great Flood? Quite likely, it would seem. Or a very similar tragedy. There is a plethora of strong literary and folkloric references (and some good hard evidence to boot) supporting the idea of periodic, cyclical and/or random earth-change catastrophes. Modern science has turned a deaf ear to such evidence because it does not fit the proper paradigms. But the evidence is old and plentiful and will not go away.

The Egyptian priest in Plato's *Timaeus* warns us of the "Many and diverse . . . destructions of mankind which have been and shall yet be; the greatest are wrought by fire and water, but there are others, slighter, wrought by countless causes." Referring to the Phaeton myth, the same priest acknowledges that it has "the semblance of a mere fable, but the fact of it is a deviation of the bodies which revolve in heaven about the earth and a destruction, coming at long intervals, of things on the earth in much fire." Finally he speaks of "when the torrents come down on you from heaven again, at the usual period, like a pestilence." Remarks such as these seem to support modern theories of killer comets and asteroids and of a potential 10th and perhaps 11th planet, a Nemesis or Marduk *or both*.

In addition to all of the above recommended items of clothing, we should not forget to include several pair of heavy wool or cotton socks, several pair of thermal underwear, several pair of warm slacks, several warm, wool, cotton or thermal shirts and several warm sweaters. Everything, it would seem, except a warm partridge in a cool pear tree. If you live by chance in a warm climate, store them away. If you live in the North woods as I do, you can wear this finery in season, replacing the worn pieces with new ones as needed. One thing for sure: You will never have time to go shopping during a season of real calamity. And, what the heck, the store may no longer be there.

Tools

A few years ago I read an appalling newspaper account of a certain kind of survivalist mentality. It was a Sunday features interview with an entrepreneur-type chap who owned all of the proper survivalist paraphernalia in camo colors and who had added a unique twist to his inventory. He was not only planning on survival but he was going to get rich as well, or so he thought, at the same time.

This fellow had purchased thousands of army surplus needles, sewing needles. "Imagine," he said, "what people will give for these. They're worth their weight in gold."

Somehow, I have the feeling that the time is near when paper money will be worthless--and gold, perhaps, as well. You cannot eat either nor drink them. Neither will give you shelter. Most likely those who covet them will do each other in, if earth changes do not get them first. There is probably no human characteristic more dangerous to those in its vicinity and more self-defeating to its possessor than greed in moments of great tribulation and stress. Luckily, those consumed by it are usually rapidly and thoroughly consumed until only ashes remain.

As for sewing needles, it would be wise to have a few on hand, even more for barter purposes, as long as the trader maintains the right attitude. But there are more essential tools that we would be wise to collect first and keep ready for building, rebuilding and repairing in the best and worst of times.

What are some of the most valuable tools to have ready for emergencies? Very basic ones. The following list may seem obvious to many, but I have learned that what is often obvious to one man is a revelation to another.

First, of course, a hatchet and an axe. Next, a bow saw, with spare blades, and a regular carpenter's saw. And let's not forget a nail hammer and a goodly supply of common nails. Or a good pair of pliers, a regular and a Phillips screwdriver, and perhaps a pipe wrench.

We might add an 8-pound sledge hammer and a few steel wedges. Although these latter tools are not primary, they are almost essential for splitting the more recalcitrant pieces of firewood.

There is a pretty good chance the earth-change survivor will find himself busy improvising and jerry-rigging, constructing and tearing apart, what is left of the world around him. Constructing an ark is definitely optional, but it is good to know that Ziusudra (the Sumerian Noah), Noah himself, as well as the Great Nazarene, were all willing and able carpenters.

All of the tools mentioned above can be purchased for a little over $100. This is not much of an expenditure compared to the amount of insurance they offer.

There are several other items which are not, strictly speaking, tools but which I consider almost essential during protracted, violent, geologic changes. First is a wood-burning stove. Pick one, whether cast iron or boiler steel, which is airtight at the seams, relatively rust free and has a flat top. With such a product, you cannot only warm yourself but cook as well. Secondly, a flashlight is fine, but sooner or later batteries grow weak. My experience suggests "sooner." Purchase a lantern that uses kerosene for fuel. Although a Coleman-type gas lantern might suffice, it is likely that kerosene will be easier to acquire than gasoline. Propane and butane refills might be even more difficult to find. The skeptic might object here and say that the last several suggestions are highly speculative. Granted, they are. To be doubly safe, it might be an excellent idea to hold a goodly number of wax candles in reserve to pinch hit for any failures in whatever you choose as your primary lighting source. Keep your candles in a cool place. High heat warps and melts them. Candles may be old-fashioned but they are very practical. Better twice careful than sorry and blind.

There are additional items that also do not qualify as

tools but which would be wise investments. For instance, a tent. Choose one that sleeps four or five people (you never know when you're going to have company). A sleeping bag or two is also a good choice. Choose one that is good to at least 30 degrees Fahrenheit. Better yet choose one that will keep you cozy at 10 degrees Fahrenheit. The subzero models are best but they are expensive. If you can afford one by all means buy it. And consider an army cot. They come in lightweight aluminum now as well as the older wood and canvas style.

Campers and outdoor types may already own most of this equipment. If so, they are one or two steps to the fore. It might be best to remember, however, that the colossally high winds and numbing cold that we can expect at times during pervasive and protracted earth changes will nullify the use of the conventional camping tent. During such winds and temperatures, would-be survivors are going to have to seek shelter below ground. The more protected the place, the better.

I have not talked much about the obverse side of the high winds-numbing cold coin. It is possible, of course, that an extraterrestrial object, such as an asteroid, large meteor or comet, impacting the planet might trigger a holocaust complete with stifling, deadly heat, deadly gases and an atmosphere so clogged with soot and particulate matter that the air would be almost unbreathable. (A discussion of breathing apparatuses appears in chapter six, "Maintaining Breathable Air".) To avoid both extremely high and abnormally low temperatures, there is nothing that beats an underground retreat. The deeper in the earth you can burrow, the safer you will be, until that happy day when surface conditions

61

return to a semblance of what we have come to think of as normal.

Pots and Pans and Sundry Items

Now let us turn at this point to a more pleasant topic, one innately close to the hearts of the Julia Childs of this world but, in this case, one even more in harmony with the thinking and practices of the legendary Ted Trueblood who wrote for several decades many memorable articles on fishing and outdoor cookery for *Field and Stream* magazine. Our topic, specifically, is the utensils best suited to prepare food either in the wild or under stressful, natural conditions.

The gung-ho survivalist maintains that he does not need utensils. That a spit can be made of a young sapling. That fingers and teeth are the original knives and forks. All true enough, but such rigorous denial is usually not absolutely necessary with a little planning.

Nothing beats the old cast-iron skillet for frying and its cousin, the cast-iron pot, for boiling and baking. Here we have both reliability and durability--and, according to some people, built-in good flavor. There are many credible outdoor types around who will swear that nothing tastes better than simple grub cooked over a wood fire in cast iron. I will not argue. Perhaps it is the ravenous appetite raised by strenuous, outdoor activity or the clean-air ambience or, more likely, the smell and seasoning of wood smoke that makes this food taste so special. Maybe there is still much in us that remembers its atavistic past. All I really know is that I have tasted cast-iron, outdoor cookery, and I have cooked with it myself, and I have no complaints. At times I have been full of compliments.

The most important consideration for the would-be cast-iron chef is to provide himself/herself at least one fry pan and one pot if possible. The pot usually comes with a wire handle spanning it and can be used atop a grill, atop strategically placed stones or hung upon a stanchion of your own choosing. It is possible to buy metal tripods manufactured for campfire cooking, but they are expensive. It is much cheaper to weld together, or have welded for you, 3 rods and a pendant hook, if you have the time and inclination for such projects.

If you choose to use aluminum, stainless steel or copper pots and pans for outdoor cooking be aware that many of the handles manufactured today are not up to the abuse of being exposed for long periods of time to direct flame. These handles often burn or melt, and the thinness of the metal bodies and handles of these pots and pans contributes to easy denting. I have, however, eaten pretty fair meals out of a dented pot, even an aluminum one. When a body is hungry, he seldom cares which blackened pot is feeding him, and, as irrational as it sounds, I am one of those subscribers to the theory that almost any food cooked in any pot or pan out-of-doors almost invariably tastes better than food cooked indoors.

Need I say it is a a good idea to stock away some durable "silverware." Plain old stainless steel will do fine, and if the Vanderbilts, Whitneys or their ilk happen to traipse through your campsite and smell your fine food a-cooking, I doubt whether they will complain about your tableware. Like the hungry Sumerian *anunnaki* ("the gods of heaven and earth") who returned to earth after the Great Flood and smelled the meat being cooked by the few human survivors, they may even gush over your wonderful cuisine. Accept the compliments graciously and, remember, if you have a tendency of any kind to feel piqued over the thought of the vast wealth such folks have accumulated in the past, forget it. Such thoughts are not worthy of you. And, chances are, whatever money they had or still carry is now useless. A campfire in times of great trouble is a great social leveler.

Another item whose survival value cannot be exaggerated is the small, portable, metal grill. These can be purchased for a few dollars at a discount house. One sure way to acquire one is to buy a cheap, charcoal-grill set. Don't, however, expect to find a ready supply of charcoal and lighter fluid during catastrophic times, but the grill itself is serviceable under even the most trying conditions as long as some type of fuel--especially wood-- is available. The edges of this grill, minus accompanying charcoal pan, can be set upon large logs or stones for support just as you might do with your cast-iron pots and pans. You then set your pots and pans directly upon the grill itself. What is more, such a grill, with several square feet of surface area, can be used to span the ground-level hole of a small, open, pit-fire.

Of all the containers you may choose to collect and keep in reserve, the most important are your water jugs. These can vary in size from Boy Scout-type or army-type canteens to 5-gallon cans or even larger plastic or metal drums. Cherish your water and what contains it. Adequate potable water is necessary to your subsistence. Your health depends on it. Polluted water in dirty, inadequate containers will spell the end of you, even if you have managed to survive earthquakes, volcanism, tornadoes, tidal waves, floods, wild animals and marauding humans.

Additional Items

There are many additional items the would-be survivor might consider having on hand during emergencies. Some of these are optional and a matter of personal taste. Others qualify as necessities. Some of the more important items to consider:

(1) First aid kit
(2) Transistor radio and spare batteries
(3) A reserve supply of any prescription medicines
(4) Flashlight and spare batteries
(5) Photovoltaic cells to recharge batteries

6

Maintaining Breathable Air

At first glance, this chapter may come as a surprise to some people. But I think you'll agree, on second thought, that during times of violent earth changes, and particularly during times of intense volcanism which is likely to occur with extreme tectonic activity, the air we breathe cannot be taken for granted.

During the eruption of Tambora on the island of Sumbawa, April 10 and 11, 1815, 92,000 people died either as a direct result of the eruption or because of conditions immediately succeeding it. Mount Tambora, which once stood at 4,300 meters above sea level, was reduced to a 6-kilometer-wide caldera at 2,850 meters above sea level. According to R. J. Blong (*Volcanic Hazards*) the explosion was heard as far away as 2,600 kilometers. This catastrophe is known to be the greatest ash eruption in the last 10,000 years (the Holocene period). The year 1816 was called "the year without a summer" in the Northern Hemisphere. This was most likely due to a drop in mean temperature, a drop which has been estimated at 0.4 degrees to 0.7 degrees Centigrade. And the drop in temperature itself has been deduced to have been caused by the tremendous amount of ash sent into the atmosphere. For 2 days after the eruption, virtual darkness covered the earth for a distance of approximately 600 kilometers from the blast site. Ash fell as far away as 1,300 kilometers, and its total volume has been estimated by R. B. Stothers at 150 kilometers *to the third power* which is twice the volume believed to have been sent skyward by the eruption of Krakatoa.

On the night of August 26-27, 1883, the small volcanic isle known as Krakatoa, located between Java and Sumatra, erupted violently. The explosion reduced the land area of the island from approximately 18 square miles to about 6 square miles. The explosion and accompanying submarine earthquake created a tidal wave estimated at its greatest height to have been 50 feet high. This wave is known to have travelled at least 8,000 miles and have killed approximately 36,000 people along the coasts of Java and Sumatra. The loudest discharge produced a noise heard as far away as 3,000 miles. The great amount of particulate matter released into the stratosphere is reported to have caused brilliant sunrises and sunsets worldwide for the next three years. D. I. Axelrod's research indicates that the mean temperature in France remained about 10 degrees Centigrade colder than normal for three years.

Axelrod also points out how lesser eruptions can severely affect local and worldwide climate. For example, solar radiation in Algeria was reduced approximately 20 per cent after the eruption of Katmai in 1912; after Bali erupted in 1960, the north-central and northeastern United States experienced a harsh winter. It is a matter of dispute how much recent eruptions such as that of Mount Saint Helens and Mount Pinatubo have affected worldwide meteorological and climatic conditions. But imagine, if you can, how much particulate matter a half dozen or more large volcanoes erupting simultaneously or successively could spew into the atmosphere in a short period of time? This is one of many possible scenarios awaiting us in the future, and it is in our best interest to acknowledge it honestly and take, if we can, appropriate evasive action.

Airborne, volcanic particulate matter, when small enough and plentiful enough, can kill. Suffocation from inhaled dust (as well as from heat and poisonous gases) is a large possibility, especially for those close to, and down wind of, an eruption. It should be noted, however, that not all eruptions issue forth particulate matter. Mount Saint Helens did. Pinatubo did. But some active volcanoes like Kilauea, and others in the Hawaiian Islands group and elsewhere in the Pacific, primarily disgorge great quantities of molten lava. Although dangerous, they are less of a potential hazard than their more explosive cousins.

There is a large probability that, during a time of great worldwide earth-change activity, many volcanoes will in fact erupt almost simultaneously. Today volcanoes in the so-called Ring of Fire, which girdles the Pacific ocean and includes those found in California, Oregon, Washington and Alaska, are becoming increasingly restless (e.g. Mount Saint Helens, Pinatubo, Mayon, Semeru, Makushin . . . .) All of these are powerful, potential arsenals of great amounts of lava and other ejecta, both large (called "bombs" and cinders) and small (ash). Anyone who has seen a reconstruction of what happened to ancient Pompeii, destroyed in 79 A.D. by one of Vesuvius' paroxysmal eruptions, will never underestimate the suffocation-quotient of this kind of natural, grim reaper. Most of the dead were found buried in grotesque postures beneath several feet of ash. Whether the residents of the city died from heat affixiation, were suffocated by ash or were killed by a combination of both, it is obvious that their end was as sudden as it was unexpected.

Would some of these people have survived if they had possessed, at the time of the catastrophe, an effective respirator? Quite possibly. A respirator might have given them the time to withdraw far enough away from the city to save themselves from the cascading, aerial fallout. And it most likely would have protected them from the poisonous gases (carbon monoxide, sulfur dioxide and other more rare, and deadly, gases) that may well have accompanied the eruption.

A respirator is, with proper filters and eye protection, a gas mask. A gas mask will not *assure* your survival when the air becomes clogged with ash and dust and filled with toxic fumes but it will *insure* it. I would rather have a serviceable respirator available than be found *in extremis* without one wishing I had one.

Where do you get such a device? You have several options. U.S. Army surplus masks are available. Some, needless to say, are quite dated, and the effectiveness of their cartridges is questionable. I do not know where you can get fresh replacements readily for these masks. Israeli surplus masks that were manufactured for the Gulf War have been, however, recently available through liquidation firms (e.g. *The Sportsman's Guide*, 441 Farwell Avenue, South, Saint Paul, MN) for as little as $10 with replacement cartridges at $5 each. These cartridges were intended to filter out nerve gas and other highly lethal toxins. Although there active life is short, 10 to 15 minutes of effectiveness with nerve gas, they should last longer against such noxious gases as sulfur dioxide and carbon monoxide. Better yet, they should work well, and for an extended period of time, as a filtering agent against ash and dust.

Is there another alternative at a reasonable price? Yes, there is. Any agricultural respirator with the right cartridge will probably do the job for you under most conditions. There are no absolute guarantees, either from me or anyone else. If someone offers you one, run from this person as fast and as far away as possible. This is a charlatan pretending to have knowledge he(or she) cannot possibly have. Neither you nor I nor anyone else can foresee the future well enough to know for certain exactly what kind of conditions will prevail at a given moment of time.

You and I are looking for a respirator with a cartridge that will protect us from fine particulate matter and acrid gases such as the sulfuric fumes which issue from many erupting volcanoes. Several firms make these masks, among them 3-M, Wilson, U.S. Safety, Moldex and Pro-Tech. The masks come in either half-mask or full mask form. The half-masks sell for between $20 and $30. The full masks cost about $100 to $200.

For protection from acrid gases most of these manufacturers recommend the yellow cartridges. These cartridges are replaceable, and you need two for the mask to work properly, one for each side of the face-piece.

They can be purchased without the mask itself, usually in boxes of two or six cartridges, for about $30. The cotton-like pre-filters, which are used in conjunction with them, are usually, but not always, included.

We must never underestimate the amount of particulate matter that multiple, volcanic eruptions can place in the atmosphere and the damage it can do. As the past has taught us (albeit on a much smaller scale), a great portion of this particulate matter will stay airborne for a year or more, cutting off the sun's rays and perhaps drastically reducing the earth's temperature. Summers and winters will be colder. Just how cold is a matter of speculation. Subzero conditions are not unlikely. Agriculture may suffer greatly under a lurid sky that suggests Wagner's *Gotterdammerung*, literally "the twilight of the gods." And, of course, twilight as well for we humans who still walk the earth and scuff the soil for our daily bread.

Actually, a similar scenario was predicted several years ago by several American scientists studying the effects, especially the atmospheric dust-cloud, that most likely would occur after the impact of a sizable extraterrestrial object such as a large asteroid, meteorite or comet. Richard Turco, Brian Toon, Thomas P. Ackerman, James B. Pollack and Carl Sagan concluded that an atmospheric dust-layer caused by such a catastrophe could impede direct sunlight from reaching the planet's surface and reduce the average surface temperature to approximately 20 degrees below freezing. Snow cover, which reflects sunlight, would hinder this light from turning into infrared heat. Some paleontologists and geologists had believed all along that a drastic climate change had killed the dinosaurs, and this kind of model fit in perfectly with such thinking.*

Toon and his associates were not, however, through theorizing. It occurred to them that a nuclear war could precipitate similar conditions. The major part of the atmospheric dust-mantel would not be raised by blast effects but by the extensive soot caused by burning cities, forests and vegetation. One analysis of their work appeared in *Science* magazine and soon became known as the TTAPS report, an acronym of their initials. Thus was born the idea of "nuclear winter," one further stern reminder that man's health is intimately related to the health of his habitat and that he has contrived, with some fickleness, the means to obliterate both.

I have already spoken of using wads of fiberglass insulation or cotton as makeshift air filters in the air-vent tubes of underground shelters (see chapter three, "Finding Adequate Shelter"). Obviously, if the outside air is constantly polluted with acrid gases we have a major, immediate, life-threatening problem. Respirators will have to be worn until such gases dissipate. If the only airborne danger, however, is from a heavy concentration of particulate matter, it is possible that we will not need to wear masks while inside our covered earth shelters. Our crude fiberglass or cotton filtration may be enough of a hedge to allow us to sleep and move around maskless. This would be no small delight compared to sleeping with a mask covering our face. Anyone who has worn any kind of respirator over an extended period of time will testify to the inconvenience. They simply are not

---

*It was Luis Alvarez who was the first to become convinced it was caused by an extraterrestrial impact.

comfortable.

I have a strong feeling that, under the kinds of conditions we have been discussing, our definition of what is and isn't delightful will radically change. We will be developing a new philosophy of life--simpler, less capricious, less perverse and illogical than our former one, one much more grateful now for basic amenities, much less likely to take anything for granted ever again, propelled by necessity to reinvent ourselves.

7

Friendly Companions

In this day and age it is still possible "to do a Walden." We can, if we like, repair to the woods to seek solace, to meditate, to live as we would. Henry David Thoreau, among other rugged self-sufficient American individualists, has shown us not only that it could be done but how. We can thank him for that ever invigorating piece of American philosophy with the simple title *Walden, or Life in the Woods*. But it is best to remember that Thoreau did not spend years living alone like a Robinson Crusoe, only a relative short time, and that when he wished the company of companions, he had a town and friends nearby. Thoreau was not a true hermit or a misanthrope, and he did not have to contend with the adversity of severe earth changes taking place about him to spoil his good time. We should all hope for such good fortune in the future.

It is too easy to romanticize going off on ones own to

the woods to escape the never ending exigencies and petty routines of modern, urban life like some contemporary reincarnation of Sinclair Lewis' Babbitt. The truth is more harsh. Most urbanites and suburbanites are not prepared by trade or temperament to do so and survive for any length of time. It isn't just that we have become softer and less self-reliant than our forebears, although good arguments could be offered in favor of such a proposition. More importantly, we are too gregarious as a species for most of us to enjoy being totally alone for long periods of time.

Good companions are a tonic to the soul. We learn from them, their successes and mistakes, as we learn from our own. But most importantly, they remind us that man's fate is most intricately and intimately intertwined with the fate of his fellows. And that is the way, it would seem, it was meant to be. We are the woven wickerwork of the Grand Conception, each cane peculiarly unique in its own way and yet vitally necessary to the Grand Design. Most of us can stand alone for a time, like a Horatio at the bridge, but not for long. One of the more fanciful ideas of the 19th century was that it was, somehow, in a kind of Matthew Arnold way, desirable or noble to stand aloof and proclaim a superiority to a sweating and imperfect world. If anything, the 20th century should have taught us by now that if we cannot work together, then we cannot long endure as either a species or as individuals. Truly, then the world cannot have, as Arnold said, "joy, nor love, nor light/Nor certitude, nor peace, nor help for pain."

I can think of nothing more terrible than to be the last living man on earth--no matter how quiet and beautiful that earth may be. We need desperately to share and laugh and sorrow together whether we realize it or not. Without companions and the give and take of relationships, without that electricity passing to and fro, we are more like dead circuit boxes, our connections having been stripped away.

In times of calamity, an individual needs, if ever he did, all the helping hands (and minds) he can find. And I mean helping hands. The lazy, the disenchanted and the bad-hearted he can do without. In a pinch these types of mortals will let him down. He/she is wise to avoid them, even in times of extreme stress and duress. Be kind, be respectful. Offer them advice, a little shared food, then send them on their way. The wrong spice spoils the stew. And one poison mushroom turns the pot deadly and can be fatal to all who sup unknowingly.

A contemporary of Henry David Thoreau wrote a short story about a kind of disturbed personality that is apropos of our concerns. The tale appears in Nathaniel Hawthorne's collection, *The Snow-Image and Other Twice Told Tales*, with the title, "The Man of Adamant." Here we find graphically illustrated an attitude which is, unfortunately, all too common in this day and age, even among some New-Agers and others who seem greatly concerned, almost overly concerned (which is possible), with surviving the coming earth changes. The kind of contemporaries I speak of, like the man of adamant in Hawthorne's story, are obsessed with their special vision of reality. Self-righteously so. Like the man of adamant, they would take themselves off to the woods, convinced their fellow men are all rotten and unworthy of their company. There they would hunker down, perhaps in an actual cave like Hawthorne's subject, to await Armageddon, general and personal annihilation, wrapping themselves in a spiritual blanket of mud that they take to be pure, unadulterated gold. These souls do not yearn for survival of either themselves or humanity. They are, in fact, acting out a death wish, alone, destitute, begrudging the spark of life in themselves and everyone else. They are, as Hawthorne indicates, an "abomination."

All of us must make certain by periodic, honest evaluations of ourselves, including our motives for our thoughts and actions, that we have not lost the vision of the inherent nobility of the human species, even though we may not always reflect that nobility as much as we would like. One of the great problems of the age has been the gnawing inferiority complex which hobbles so much of humanity. It is the other side of the Janus coin. On one side we are faced with those who are convinced they know all; on the other, and etched even more prominently, we see the picture of a humanity woefully uncertain of itself. And is it any wonder? Orthodox religion, conventional psychology and psychiatry, formal education and the mass media, not to mention the politicians, conspire noisily to remind us how doomed, mixed-up, ignorant and ignoble we are. Despite such programming, we must rediscover our worth and maintain it against all future assaults. A man who cannot shepherd himself is always at the mercy of the wolf.

Friends, first and foremost, are our closest link to the Greater Creation which enfolds us and in which we have our primary (and probably only) existence. They are clay of our clay, flesh of our flesh, blood of our blood. When we finally become thoroughly convinced of this, all thoughts of violent acts against them, our fellow beings, become, if not unthinkable, at the very least totally unacceptable. To injure them, we discover, is to wound

77

ourselves. To cut ourselves off willingly from contact with all other human beings is not natural and in most cases is pathological. It leads quickly to the atrophying of our life spirit and a gradual denudation of all civilizing influences which mark us apart from the other higher animals. This is a return to a heart of darkness that is counter to natural cosmic evolution. The man who insists on pursuing this kind of course is usually not long for this world ("'Mistah Kurtz-he dead.'").*

Friends, we discover, are our mirror selves. They multiply us. They give us energy, just as we, with our friendship, energize them. They complete us in ways we could never accomplish by ourselves. They are satellites which help light our path. Alone, we shine. But even the strongest of us will gradually wane and extinguish ourselves unless we are replenished by the affection of those about us. Alone, and without the love of others, we aren't going to make it. Alone and unable to love because of a hard heart, we doom ourselves and perhaps others as well. We become an abomination within the Grand Design. Nature has no more use for us and spits us out and casts us away until we can be recycled into a more sanguineous, amenable, respectful form.

A little logical thinking will quickly remind us of all the practical reasons why we need friends around us. Most obvious is the fact that we need their various skills. One friend may be a carpenter; another a stonemason. Yet another may be exceptionally adept at jerry-rigging electrical circuitry. Still another may be a knowledgeable

---

*Kurtz, in Joseph Conrad's novel, *Heart of Darkness,* reverts to savagery in the jungles of Africa and the reversion destroys him. The film, *Apocalypse Now,* set during the Vietnam War, visually describes a similar descent.

horticulturists. We are most likely going to be involved in growing all or part of our own food (see chapter nine, "Maintaining an Adequate Food Supply"), and we need those who have gardening knowledge and agricultural abilities around us.

Everyone has talents. Some have indisputably more than others. Whether we choose to live a communal, Fourier-type existence or live at some distance from neighbors and friends, we are going to need the talents and prowess of these people, just as they are going to need whatever help we can offer. Sharing is a concept that we in modern America have much ignored. We have been too ready to misuse and abuse such concepts as Self-Reliance and Rugged Individualism to justify all kinds of selfishness, greed and egocentricity. Now, as we face the future, our cities and villages are filled with violent crime. Not only crime against property but violence directed against one another. If we are to prevail during hard times, and avoid a *Planet of the Apes* scenario, we must recapture the trust and respect of others of an earlier time. The alternative is to run the risk of reducing ourselves to predatory animals, each out for what he can get at all costs. This kind of *modus operandi* will not work among survivors. They must learn to ban together or succumb to not only the furious elements but to the fury generated within the darker side of human nature.

Even Robinson Crusoe had his Friday. And desperately needed him. As ingenious as he was in providing for himself, he yearned for companionship. And this yearning is natural. I repeat what I have already said. Man is an inherently gregarious creature. He needs not only a mate of the opposite sex to thrive but other companions as well if he is to grow spiritually and mentally. And he needs all the friends he can get if he is to survive the present and future catastrophic earth changes.

All survivors, whether living commune-style or in separate, family-style groupings somewhat removed from their neighbors, must make preparations to defend themselves from marauding, predatory humans who have not recognized the necessity of cooperation. I have addressed this problem in the chapter "Maintaining An Adequate Defense" and will, therefore, refrain at this time from making further comments.

It is most important to realize that everyone can contribute something to the survival of those around him/her. One does not need great talents. In fact, one needs no special talents at all, only a willingness to pitch in and help with the problems at hand. As an old adage, worthy of the most Puritan-minded, states, "He who is willing to work will not remain long idle." Not during earth-change times . There will be much to do, and much that will, at any rate, be raw, physical labor. Those who have a strong back and a storehouse of energy will be valued members of any band of mortals seeking to survive in peace.

Any random selection of human beings will have a cross section of personality types. There will be the introverted and the extroverted. The intellectually inclined and the more basic, down-to-earth pragmatists. Even the comedians and the curmudgeons. It is true, as we have been often told, that adversity has a way of bringing out the best and worst in people. The sunny side of this truism is that stressful situations usually facilitate the emergence of natural leaders. It will be the task of these incipient leaders to bring order and organization to what may appear in the beginning as pure chaos.

One thing seems predictable. Those of calmer temperament, whether living on their own or as part of a larger community, will weather the various storms of earth change and interpersonal adjustment more successfully than those who will not, or cannot, control their emotions. And those with a sense of humor may come to feel especially blessed. There is no human trait more valuable--and more pleasant with which to be associated-- than a good sense of humor when it comes to meeting adversity head-on and looking it straight in the eye. As an Ozark native once put it, "A man ain't nothing if he doesn't tickle."

As a youth I wasn't without a sense of humor, although I haven't the faintest idea where it came from, unless it was the stepchild of necessity. I have often thought as the years passed that it was probably in great measure because of this trait that I survived myself. Early on I realized we were a dysfunctional family but a very private one at that. Neither my mother nor my father would ever admit to this failing and certainly I, as a self-conscious child, did not want them publicizing the fact. The thought of such a thing was enough to bring on huge waves of shame that rolled over me and threatened to drown me. This was long before people looked forward to talking smugly about their various afflictions and sundry treatments at cocktail parties and other public gatherings. Afflictions of a psychological nature just weren't talked about.

It isn't surprising that I became extremely introverted. I was, after all, an only child. Socializing was dreadful, the pain almost unbearable. I realized the value of having friends but the act of making friends was nerve-wracking. It was simply too fearsome an experience for me and I avoided it when possible.

As I grew out of my teens, I forced myself to be a more public figure. I adopted masks and wore them to face the world. They were a kind of armor which made the theater of life more bearable. One could change masks as the situation demanded. I believe many of my acquaintances also adopted masks. We were so many scared characters in search of a play and dreading we would find it.

Sometimes the masks I wore were quite convincing. I could for a time adopt them, accept them, in fact became quite enthralled with them. I learned it was easy to fool many people into thinking I was someone I was not. This taught me how easily misled people are, and I began to realize how dangerous it was to do so. All the same, I was still lonely although a little less terrified.

In time I learned a different way. I developed my own voice. Most of the awkwardness disappeared with more experience, as it is wont to do. Friendship, honest friendship, now comes more easily as the old learning, the old programming, gives way to the new. I now know and appreciate how strong the human inclination is to be around one's own kind. I can imagine nothing so lonely as to be totally bereft of one's own kind. That would be true bereavement, a state we all should hope never becomes our own. It may be the only true hell--which goes by so many other names--on earth or in heaven.

Why do I tell you this? Because I have learned that new friends are like a good beaujolais. They should be appreciated in the present, celebrated now. Old friends are like good champagne. They are excellent now and grow better with age. Let us hope in a time of great earth changes that we will have both kinds around us, offering us encouragement and their support as we build a new world out of the old.

8

The Importance of Community

Many friends working together for the common good make the ideal community. Whether there are many such communities now in this world, untainted by such vices as unbirdled personal ambition and general avarice, is not the point. What is vitally important is the need for such communities in an earth-changed, ravaged world.

Long-term survival of the individual will depend, in large measure, on whether that individual is able and willing to assimilate himself(herself) to a compatible group, all of whose members wish each other well and are themselves each individually willing to work for the common welfare. An organ transplant analogy is not out of place here. If the individual survivor is not compatible with the group that receives him, or is rejected by that group outright, he(she) had best look immediately elsewhere for a group which is more in sympathy with his(her) disposition and interests. Chances are he(she) will find what they are looking for. Square pegs don't fit round holes although there is nothing wrong with being either.

How does community happen? Certainly not by accident. Definitely by will power and need. And loneliness.

In a changed world bereft of many, if not all, of its former institutions (not to mention creature comforts)--without public utilities to supply energy, without the food distribution system we have come to depend on, probably without police protection to control the unruly--the local, reformed community will become of vital importance.

What might this community look like? And what will its functions be?

Practically speaking, this new community will be an extension of the individual, just as the old community was, but most probably on a much smaller scale. It will consist of individuals and families who find themselves occupying contiguous territory or even the same territory. These will be the survivors of cataclysm. Some will find themselves hundreds of miles from their old home territory. They will now be true pioneers, from near and far. The trigger mechanisms which will make these strangers coalesce and find comfort in one another will be several. I have already mentioned the two most obvious: (1) need and (2) the natural desire for human companionship.

Some communities most likely will be very small. Perhaps only a few individuals helping each other. Others may be much larger, a number of individuals and families naturally gravitating together to make life easier.

It can be expected that certain natural leaders will arise. These will be recognized by the community for their outstanding qualities and abilities and be asked by consensus to serve in various capacities: food production, education, protection . . . . We all have some talents, and it will be up to the members of the new communities to recognize those talents in each other and put them to use, with the willing consent, of course, of the possessors of those talents. Successful communities of the future, especially those burdened by the stress of violent earth changes, must depend on the free will and good will of their members. Without either, human chaos will swiftly follow the natural chaos of the environment. The slow moral degeneration of society today can, in fact, be partially imputed to an ever increasing lack of good will, and the concomitant distrust that goes along with it, among the members of contemporaneous society. Violence seldom occurs among those who respect each other and wish one another well.

When successful present-day communal enterprises are looked at, such as Findhorn in England, several reasons for their success seem most salient. Most noticeable is the encouragement that each individual member is given to choose work which he likes in a field in which he has some expertise. It might be added that the truly lazy, the real hanger-on type, is not tolerated. Those who are too lazy to raise their arms to feed themselves are encouraged in a friendly but firm fashion to raise their feet in successive steps down the road. This is neither cruel nor unfeeling behavior but necessary and practical. Those who are truly able to support themselves have been encouraged to do so while remaining all the while part of the community. These individuals have almost always been willing to share whatever excess they have. Such dispositions of labor and such sharing will most likely be the hallmarks of the successful, small, survival community of the future--just as they are today in similar communities which outlasted the mushroom-like explosion and fungal decay of so many disorganized "hippie" communes of the '60s. The formula for success, then, seems to have two main ingredients: first, the striving for individual self-sufficiency, then the sharing of excess bounty.

Obviously, none of us can be completely self-sufficient or as thoroughly organized as we would like to be, even if we have dutifully read Emerson and Franklin and done our best to imitate their good advice, or diligently studied Fourier or the New Harmony experiment. Some of us are better at one thing, some at another. Here is where a simple division of labor naturally occurs. The wise neo-society will take gentle advantage of this natural situation for the benefit of both the individual and the community.

If Tom makes good shoes and Sally makes good shirts, there will undoubtedly come a day when Tom wants a shirt and Sally is willing to trade one for a pair of shoes. Bartering is an ancient form of commerce. In a time of great earth changes, it will probably become the main form of commerce. Bartering, or simple trading, is the original and most natural way of doing business. The advent of coinage, with artificially induced fluctuations in value, has caused the "civilized" world much grief--and worked to the disadvantage of the poor and less devious-minded.

Massive earth changes will most likely force the greater proportion of surviving humans into an agriculturally-based lifestyle such as existed in America prior to the First World War. This will be a social, economic and psychological boon rather the the blight it first might appear to be.

If a community has enough members, the process of field work, that is, gardening for subsistence, will be much easier. The more hands available to hoe, the more certain an adequate food supply (see chapter nine, "Maintaining an Adequate Food Supply"). Food will be the dominant necessity, the overriding thought that will almost obsess the lives of all survivors in the days immediately following massive earth changes. Once individuals, and community members working in concert, have assured themselves of a nutritious and somewhat varied diet through hard work, barter and trade, they can concentrate more of their energy on providing structured educational opportunities for both children and adults (see chapter eight, "The Importance of Community") and preserving other vestiges of more civilized living (see chapter twelve, "Maintaining the Rudiments of Civilization"). In the earliest days of survival-living, unfortunately, some exigencies must take precedence over others before a more traditionally civilized state of affairs can reign.

It is imperative that each community, whether made up of members inhabiting the same grounds or composed of a more loose-knit confederation of local individuals and families, make some preparations to defend themselves from marauding bands (or marauding individuals) out to get whatever they can however they can (see chapter eleven, "Maintaining an Adequate Defense"). A warning device such as a church bell, or other object capable of giving a loud, prolonged warning noise, is desirable. If this kind of thinking seems simplistic to you, not worthy of civilized behavior and a throwback to the wild West mentality, do not be deceived. Catastrophic earth changes are capable of creating a desperate, even vicious type of scavenger that would make Billy the Kid and the

James boys seem tame.

There must be, at any rate, some agreed upon way, either by signal or messenger, for community members, or friends, to come to one anothers aid in times of danger. This system, whatever its nature, must be capable of being activated rapidly. And the "defenders" must always remain just that--defenders, ready to use no more force than is absolutely necessary to quell whatever disturbance is threatening the community.

Our modern sociologists tell us that it was from the "social contract" between families that the tribes and finally the nations grew. This contract has been, it would seem, and continues to be, undermined by the more aggressive and selfish human characteristics. It is a large question whether humanity will be able to overcome in the near future pronounced, active tendencies which are divisive and destructive and work against an even closer alignment of humanity into something approaching a world government. This is the same idea, of course, as the projected New World Order that, by dire necessity, we are presently moving haltingly toward. It is an idea which scares some people but one which is inevitable if the world should last so long.

If we should last so long.

Massive earth changes, if they occur, will radically alter the prospects for a world government in the foreseeable future.* It should be rather obvious to us now, after the passage of untold centuries of strife, that if the human species on planet Earth is to survive future

---

*So, of course, could nuclear war or a combination of war and massive earth changes.

cataclysms, even a remnant of the species, it must adopt a more pacific attitude in general. It must cast away military armaments and even the thought of such armaments. It must truly beat swords into plowshares if it is going to have any chance whatsoever of surviving, because all the energy the survivor can muster is going to be needed to insure survival. There will be none to spare. Those who insist upon living by the sword will consume themselves and others like themselves. This is not just biblical prophecy but, if we stop to think carefully about it, logically predictable, a probability with a very high chance of becoming an actuality.

It may well take the misfortune of catastrophic natural events to make the surviving remnants of humanity realize, in moments of retrospection, that warfare is, and always has been, a special kind of human dementia that serves only to destroy true community and true communion among men. Our destiny as a species is together--not as isolated individual entities romanticizing ourselves as self-sufficient islands unto ourselves or as self-righteous nations set against each other.

When enough survivors have finally become convinced that peaceful living is the only sane lifestyle, and the only truly productive one, then a real new world order will be possible. Then, as new community melds with new community and a new nation and world is born, the scourges of the old way of living, such as personal aggressiveness and societal warfare, will have been cured by the magical elixir of human understanding. And human understanding, we will have learned, leads inevitably, though sometimes slowly, to brotherly love.

Brotherly love is one of the most talked about and least understood ideas in the world today. To understand it, we must recognize the stranger as ourselves in disguise. This we refuse to do because of confused, misled thinking, much of it caused by formal education and the malignant influence of other informal teachers. It may take the shock of violent earth-change circumstances to clear our heads and open our hearts. Like good cream, the lovers will rise to the surface. The haters and deniers will sink away into that special self-made hell they have created for themselves and others like them.

9

Maintaining an Adequate Food Supply

Ah, to plant a seed! To watch it sprout! All my life I have been a planter of things. Even as a city dweller I spaded and weeded, turning one entire backyard into a miniature orchard of apple, pear and cherry trees. I also constructed a vegetable garden of raised beds in that same backyard, much to the amusement of some of my neighbors and the consternation of others.

As a boy I was always a catcher of butterflies, a collector of toads and angleworms, a snipper of flowers both wild and domesticated. At the age of six, I neatly cropped my neighbors' zinnias, cosmos and dahlias, bundled them in neat bouquets, stashed them in my Radio Flyer, hauled them to the nearest street corner and sold them to passing motorists which included, much to my surprise, several of those neighbors. Needless to say, I got found out. There was some noise, and I long carried with me the memory of the shame of having pointed out to me the crime I had committed.

But I have never had to regret planting a single seed. And I have continued to plant, through bountiful seasons and lean years--it made no real difference to me. I planted regardless, come rain, hail or drought, and never regretted a moment. The reward was as much in the act as the harvest itself, and I can honestly say I have learned many things about the secrets of life from watching my seeds and hoeing my rows that I could not have learned nearly so well any other way.

Now, as the seasons of life come full circle, I find myself no longer a young man. But I "work" my 1200 fruit trees ungrudgingly and watch over my large garden with gladness. Never, ever, even when arm muscles ache and my back objects, does my mind and spirit rebel against such a pursuit. No regrets here. To the contrary. I am healthier and wiser for my efforts--and, as an added bonus, better fed than most.

And yet, in the back of my mind, I have continually held a thought. What if, I wondered, this gardening was a matter of life and death? What if earth changes occur which are so severe that gardening is no longer a hobby and pleasure but becomes instead pure necessity? Would I, will I, still rejoice in it? Or will I come to dread it as a drudgery I cannot do without?

I cannot answer these questions. I have not been in a position where I have had to. But, as the old-time gardeners say, the signs are not good. Perhaps I should prepare myself for the worst while hoping for the best. Perhaps you should as well.

What does the earth-change survivor need to know about rising produce to feed himself? A great deal. But a willing disposition is most important. Without it he doesn't have a fly-catcher's chance in a month of Sundays.

In the beginning were heaven and earth and the elements. We do not have, and never had, much control of them. We cannot bend the wind or command the rain or divert the fallout after massive volcanism. We can, however, store away a supply of basic tools, seeds and foodstuffs which will help us get started when starting is possible. We have forgotten in these times of plenty that it is wise to set aside provisions for the times of famine. There are few Josephs (Genesis 41) to advise our present-day pharaohs. And fewer leaders who will listen to the warnings.

The most basic tools of subsistence gardening are a spade and a hoe. Without these, no nonmechanical gardening can take place. The cost of these tools is slight, there practical value great. If you have no use for them now, store them away. They may become someday the most important possessions you own. Literally worth more than their weight in platinum. We must keep in mind that during catastrophic times you cannot eat platinum. It becomes virtually useless. You are better off with simple tools. Place your faith in them and let the hoarders of gold and silver and other formerly precious things discover how useless and worthless nonutilitarian stuffs can be.

After you break the ground and level it, you need something to plant. What seeds make most sense? Although this is a question easily equivocated, I think good old-fashioned common sense can go a long way toward answering it. I do not pretend to have the definitive answer. I don't think there is one. Different people will have different preferences with good, logical reasons for their choices, but several strong arguments can be given for the following selection which is most likely to do well in specific, less than ideal, circumstances.

First, however, let's reiterate a few projections we have made about the climatic conditions which may prevail in the near future in North America and other parts of the world. Our selection of seeds is vitally connected to these projections.

With massive earth changes high winds can be expected. Possibly these winds will be of hurricane force or greater. At the same time, we can expect heavily polluted air which will cause the average temperature of the earth to decline. Less sunlight, less photosynthesis. This means all trees and plants, including all edible species, will grow more slowly. Many may die, as has often happened at the boundary lines separating geologic epochs of the past. In many, if not all, parts of the world, we can expect an abbreviated growing season.

It is difficult to project what effects radical weather changes alone will have on worldwide food production, which even now has been badly compromised in Russia, Japan, India, China, Bangladesh and in the Sahel and Horn areas of Africa. But the dictum stated earlier, that it is wise to be prepared for the worst, would especially seem to apply here. It might well be best not to know clairvoyantly or otherwise exactly, precisely what the worst will be. Then we do not so much run the risk of underestimating and underplanning, because human nature has the curious habit of discounting the inevitable, even when the inevitable has been made graphically evident.

Let's narrow our scope, clarify our focus once again. A large challenge is often best met with an attention to small details. To neglect tying down one stitch is to risk the unraveling of the entire fabric of our endeavor. Part of our endeavor is to choose seeds which will better assure our survival. Especially seeds that might sprout and prosper in high winds, less sunlight than usual and cooler temperatures.

Quite possibly our most logical choices should be vegetables that produce part or all of their edible portion below ground. This leads us naturally to potatoes, turnips, beets, radishes, carrots and kohlrabi. All are resistant to normal wind damage. All are cold hardy, doing well in daytime temperatures of around 60 degrees. Most potatoes will mature in 70 to 100 days. Turnips, beets, carrots and kohlrabi will mature in normal years in about 60 days, which is a relatively short growing season. (Add some days to maturity if sunlight is less than normal.) Radishes are quite quick, real speed-runners, and can be counted on to produce edible tubers in 20 to 30 days under normal conditions.

The main obstacle I can foresee in raising these particular vegetables would be excessively high wind. The growing tops--which in the case of turnips, beets, radishes and kohlrabi are quite edible--might be damaged, even to the point where not enough foliage remains to bring the species to maturity. Consider planting such plants close to walls, large rocks or other structures which will offer some protection from high velocity wind currents.

One way to cushion the effects of high wind and low temperature is to dig a pit garden, as is the practice in some parts of China. A pit garden is exactly what it sounds like. Usually a large square or rectangular excavation is dug several feet into the ground, often below the depth of the average frost line. The pit should not be so deep as to dramatically affect the amount of sunlight reaching the good ground soil at its bottom. Naturally the taller the surrounding walls, the more shading that will occur. A pit 3 to 4 feet deep generally should be quite adequate, which is the maximum depth of the frost line in most northern American states during an average winter. The primary advantage of such a structure is the extended growing season it offers, not a little consideration in times of food scarcity.

The pit garden can be covered with plastic held down by large stones, boards or earth. It can also be covered with old storm windows or acrylic panels, the latter available from building supply companies. The acrylic panels have the advantage of not shattering but the disadvantage of being hard to find in times of social and natural turmoil. Buy them and use them or store them away somewhere prior to the predictable social chaos that will result from massive earth changes.

Another way to protect limited growing areas is to use cold frames. The four sides of these are usually constructed of wood and the tops, angled toward the sun, can be covered, like the pit garden, with plastic, old windows or acrylic panels. Cold frames, however, although of low profile, are not as wind resistant as pit gardens.

I will not go into an elaborate description here of the niceties of cold-frame construction. This would take some time and, I believe, the reader is better served if I concentrate in more detail on other subjects that deserve our attention. I would refer the reader-survivalist to the myriad gardening books and magazines on such subjects and encourage some careful reading. An hour or two of quiet study in pursuit of such knowledge is much preferable to a last minute mad scramble for information when the elements are raging and libraries and bookstores everywhere are rubble. Then the only hope may be to find a knowledgeable gardening friend who is willing to share his/her experience. Why chance it? This friend may be elsewhere at the time of need or too busy with personal problems to offer much assistance.

One genus of vegetables which is quite cold hardy and should be given careful consideration is the *Brassicas*: including broccoli (*Brassica oleracea* var. *italica*), cauliflower (*Brassica oleracea* var. *Botrytis*), cabbage (*Brassica oleracea* var. *capitata*), collards (*Brassica oleracea* var. *acephala*), kohlrabi (*Brassica oleracea*) and mustard (*Brassica*). The greatest problem with these well known domesticated edibles is that direct seeding into the garden in cold climates can be risky. This problem can be solved by germinating the seeds in a cold frame until they are several inches high and then carefully transplanting them into the garden. Another potential problem is the large leaf area of most varieties. This makes them susceptible to high wind damage.

The onion genus (*Allium Cepa*) has the advantage of narrow stems and even, as do the *Brassicas*, edible stems. But it is the tumescent, tender bulb at the end of the stem of most species that attracts the gourmet and is of interest to the subsistence gardener. There are many types of onions, some bunching like Egyptian (winter) onions, and many that need more space to individually flourish. Shallots, leeks and chives are especially tender, mild forms of the onion genus, garlic a more pungent form. Don't expect large bulbs from directly seeding varieties, unless you are willing to overwinter the first year's small bulbs (of large bulb-types like Ebenezer or Stuttgarter) and transplant them the following spring.

Anyone contemplating feeding himself would do well not to forget lettuce and spinach. Most popular lettuces, such as Blackseeded Simpson and Grand Rapids, are ready for picking in approximately 40 days. They, like spinach, can be sown early in soil that is still quite cold. And if you let some of the plants go to seed, you can harvest and save this seed for next year's crop.

The earth-change survivor has no choice but to save seed. This makes it extremely important that nonhybrid species of vegetables be planted when at all possible. Open-pollinated plants produce seed that will reproduce "true." This is not the case with hybrid varieties. Some will not produce seed at all under normal gardening conditions, and whatever seed is produced will not reflect the qualities of the original hybrid.

Many gardeners love their tomatoes, beans and squash. We know from our colonial history that some North American Indian tribes planted squash among their corn hills, as do many Central American farmers to this day. The problem with tomatoes, corn and squash, and with beans also, is that all of these crops demand warm weather to really produce well. They are all particularly vulnerable and, under harsh conditions of cold weather and high winds, can be expected to produce little or nothing. Tomatoes and corn are especially finicky about getting the right amount of water at the right time. Tomatoes like a steady supply, not too little, not too much. This is a hard requirement to meet during times of rapidly fluctuating weather patterns.

It is possible, however, to plant nonhybridized species of these vegetables and have good luck saving seeds, as long as the weather will cooperate. Tomato varieties such as Rutgers and Marglobe lend themselves well to this practice and will yield seeds that will come true the next time around. Rutgers, for a nonhybrid, is a real champion, producing fine, sweet, medium-sized fruit. The plants have good natural genetic resistance to common viral and bacterial diseases.

Most popular squash are nonhybrid varieties, and seed can be easily saved which will come "true." The problem with saving squash seed, as with saving any open-pollinated species, is that if two or more varieties are planted too close to one another, they tend to interpollinate. This leaves the gardener who saves seeds wondering what "new" kind of specimens he will be mother-fathering the next year. These crossbreeds usually are quite edible, however, and it isn't likely that most hungry earth-change survivors are going to be complaining about nature's experimentation. If the gardener wishes to protect his varieties from cross-pollinating, he had best separate them by 20 to 30 feet or more.

Most green bean varieties will also produce seed which will be close to last years original, unless several varieties, as in the case with squash and corn, are allowed to cross-pollinate. Even here, as with the other species, the "new" green beans are usually quite tasty. If the gardener has spare time on his/her hands, with all the other demands of survivalist living pressing in upon him, he can sit himself down for a moment or two and have some fun naming his new crossbred variety(s). Possibly, if his sense of humor is exceptionally ripe, he can come up with names as appropriate as "Desperation," "Tasty Surprise," "Thank God It Bloomed" or even better, more thrilling, ones.

There is a bit of art in saving seeds whether that seed comes from commercial varieties or is wild-found. The three most important considerations are (1) to take the seed at the right time, (2) to dry it properly and (3) to store it properly. With lettuce, for instance, it is necessary to let the mature plant make seed. That seed should not be picked until the plant is completely through its cycle of growth and the seed has hardened. With green beans, the gardener can leave some pods unpicked. When the pods have dried out naturally on the vine, he can then remove the beans from the pods, making sure they too are dry, and store them. With a vegetable like tomatoes, it is necessary to break apart a ripe specimen, separate the seeds from the surrounding fibrous mass and then dry them carefully on a plate or in a pan.* If you insist on taking seeds from overly "green" fruits and vegetables, you will normally have little luck trying to germinate them the following spring. Vegetable seeds need a minimum time to gestate before becoming viable, as does the child in the womb. Trying to hurry the process will not work.

Once seeds are taken, it is necessary to make sure they are thoroughly dry, otherwise they are likely to mildew or rot in captivity. Place them out of direct sunlight in an area with good air circulation for several weeks until their outer surfaces have lost all tackiness. Then put them in a jar or plastic bag. Make sure the lid on any container you choose is completely airtight. One way to do this is similar to the previously discussed method of storing emergency foodstuffs. Place a piece of Saran wrap or similar material over the jar mouth and then screw on the

*Actually the tomato is not a true vegatable but a berry.

lid. Keep your seeds permanently out of the sun. A cool, dark place will make them happy until planting time. Actually, the seeds of most vegetable varieties will keep at least several years if properly cared for, although varieties do vary greatly as to the maximum number of years they will remain viable.

If by some chance, because of an axis shift or because of other earth changes, we in the United States find ourselves basking (sweating?) in a tropical environment, then such vegetables as tomatoes and melons may do gloriously well--provided that there is enough moisture accompanying the heat wave and not too much wind. Chances are, however, the climate from one region to another will show some variation as it does now, perhaps a great deal of it. It is obviously impossible to predict what conditions will obtain where. We had also better add "when." It is rather annoying to see all the new self-proclaimed prophets rising up helter-skelter who adamantly insist they are privy to the hour-and-second arrival of Wormwood, Armageddon et cetera (remember Hawthorne's "The Man of Adamant"?) and yet whose own lives are in such confusion that they have difficulty telling you the time of day.

We are surrounded today with would-be false prophets. Those, you might say, who would sell you bad seed and a psychologically disturbed jungle in which to plant it. Following the wrong piper could be as disastrous as remaining oblivious to the present signs of great social and natural change taking place about us. Protect yourself as you would the seed which feeds you. Those who would importune you too hastily and too loudly may not have your best interest at heart.

Earthquake Vulnerability

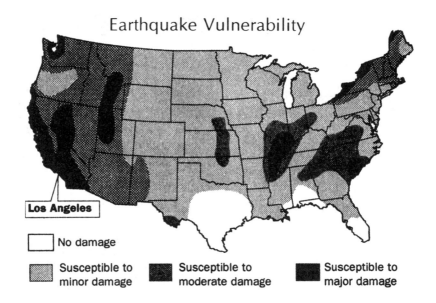

Los Angeles

☐ No damage

▨ Susceptible to minor damage

▨ Susceptible to moderate damage

■ Susceptible to major damage

Some areas have had traditionally a high susceptibility to damage.
Source (map): National Academy of Sciences.

MAJOR UNITED STATES EARTHQUAKES

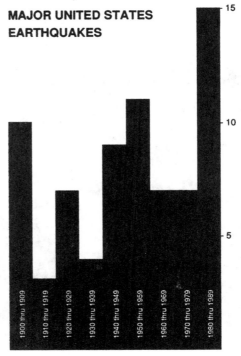

Source: U. S. Geological Survey.

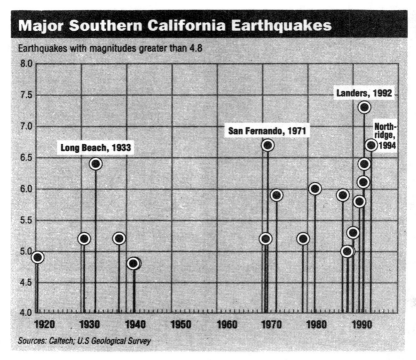

Major Southern California Earthquakes

Earthquakes with magnitudes greater than 4.8

Sources: Caltech; U.S Geological Survey

Sources: Caltech; U. S. Geological Survey.

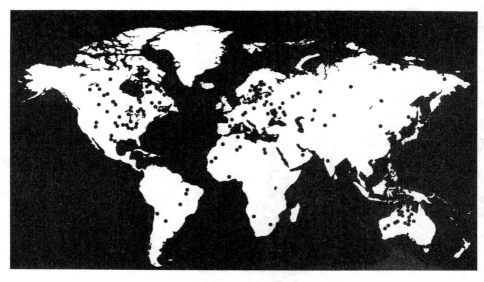

Map shows impact structures known as of 1989. Density here is a function of where most research has been done. Obviously, there are a great many astroblemes below the oceans' surfaces, although none has been found. Source: U. S. Geological Survey.

Mount Saint Helens eruption. Much ash was hoisted into stratosphere but low sulphur content reduced its ability to cause a lasting climate-altering effect. Photo: U. S. Geological Survey.

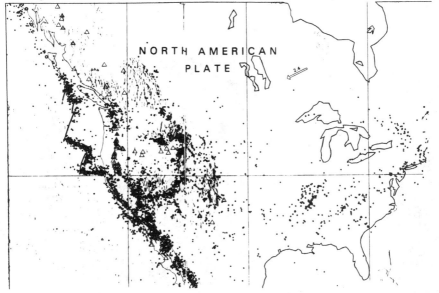

North American crustal plate showing earthquake epicenters (dots) and volcanoes (triangles). Map reproduced from an article, "This Dynamic Planet: A World Map of Volcanoes, Earthquakes and Plate Tectonics," by Tom Simkin, R. I. Tilling, J. N. Taggart, W. J. Jones and Henry Spall, 1989. Source: U. S. Geological Survey.

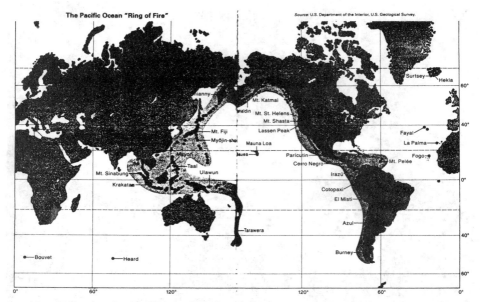

Map indicating Pacific "Ring of Fire" and the location of some of its more active and/or dangerous volcanoes. Source: U. S. Geological Survey.

My brother-in-law, Joe, standing before the entrance to the earth shelter/root cellar I built on a budget.

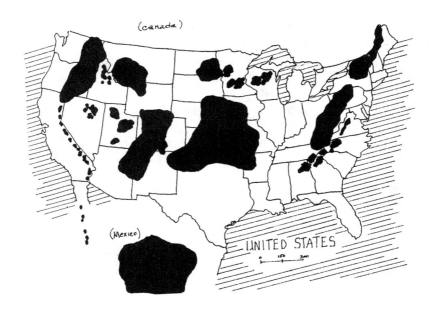

This map shows the North American continent after the Earth shift.
Striped lines are existing large water masses. White areas are existing
land. Black areas are remaining land that will be above water after the
Earth shift.

Source: map and caption courtesy of Dolores Cannon and Ozark
Mountain Publishers.

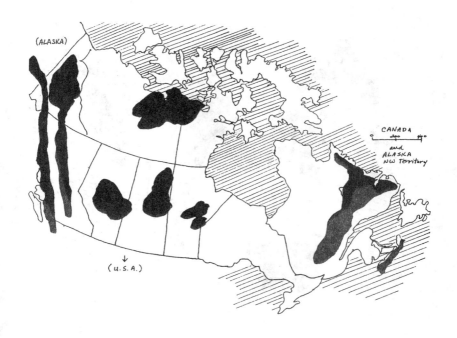

This map shows the Canada and Alaska after the Earth shift. Striped lines are existing large water masses. White areas are existing land. Black areas are remaining land that will be above water after the Earth shift.

Source: map and caption courtesy of Dolores Cannon and Ozark Mountain Publishers.

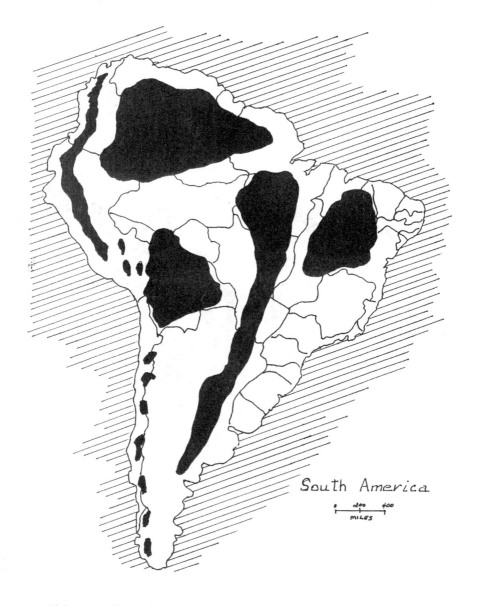

South America

0   200   400
    MILES

This map shows the South American continent after the Earth shift. Striped lines are existing large water masses. White areas are existing land. Black areas are remaining land that will be above water after the Earth shift.

Source: map and caption courtesy of Dolores Cannon and Ozark Mountain Publishers.

This map shows the European continent after the Earth shift. Striped lines are existing large water masses. White areas are existing land. Black areas are remaining land that will be above water after the Earth shift.

Source: map and caption courtesy of Dolores Cannon and Ozark Mountain Publishers.

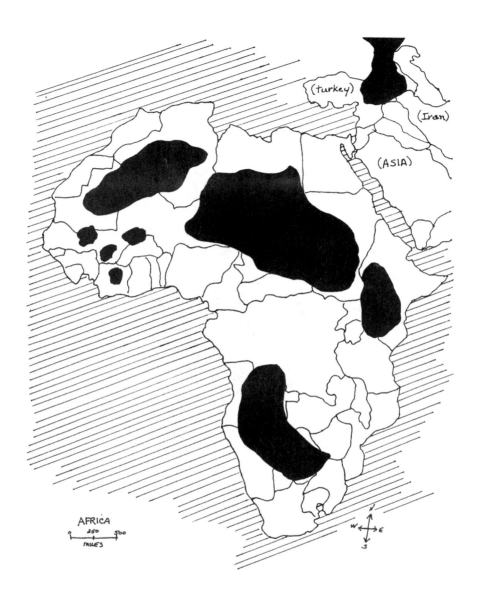

(turkey)

(Iran)

(ASIA)

AFRICA

0   250   500

MILES

N

W ← → E

S

This map shows the African continent after the Earth shift. Striped lines are existing large water masses. White areas are existing land. Black areas are remaining land that will be above water after the Earth shift.

Source: map and caption courtesy of Dolores Cannon and Ozark Mountain Publishers.

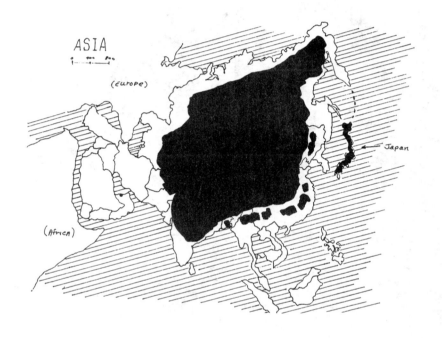

This map shows the Asian continent after the Earth shift. Striped lines are existing large water masses. White areas are existing land. Black areas are remaining land that will be above water after the Earth shift.

Source: map and caption courtesy of Dolores Cannon and Ozark Mountain Publishers.

Indian flood of 1978. Photo: courtesy of CARE.

Devastating Guatemalan earthquake of 1976 which produced 22,778 fatalities. Photo: courtesy of CARE.

Nicaraguan earthquake of 1972 which killed over 5,000 people.
Photo: courtesy of CARE.

Killer Bangladesh cyclone of 1991 resulting in many casualties.
Photo: by Shahedul Alom, courtesy of CARE.

Catastrophic Armenian earthquake of 1988 that resulted in over 55,000 deaths. Photo: courtesy of CARE.

Survivors of the initial eruption of Mount Pinatubo in the Philippines (1991) improvise living quarters. Photo: courtesy of CARE.

Some of the wreckage caused by the hurricane which struck
Honduras in 1974, causing many casualties.   Photo: courtesy of
CARE.

Indian cyclone of 1978 caused widespread damage and death within
its path. Photo: courtesy of CARE.

Some of the damage after the killer-quake of September, 1993, that killed between 10,000 and 30,000 Indians, depending on which estimate is used. Photo: courtesy of CARE.

The author digging potatoes, a crop which is cold hardy and somewhat wind resistant.

10

Foraging, Gathering, Hunting, Fishing

A sure way to keep starvation at bay is to learn to recognize the many wild, edible plants that surround us. I recall with pleasure the foraging trip taken by Euell Gibbons years ago to a vacant lot in inner-city Chicago. He made the trip to prove a point: Even in a city that prided itself on its display of concrete and steel, he could still find tasty, wild fare and could feed himself adequately with it if need be.

The sad truth is the extent to which we have become detached from the flora and fauna which is all around us and, indeed, makes up the greater natural environment of which we are a part and which we have ignored to the point of imperiling ourselves. Today the average American would be hard put to identify most species of trees and bushes which encompass him within the city and without. And as for naming the plants and grasses, wildflowers and "weeds," which are under his feet and so often brush his leg--forget it. The average city dweller can name a "weed" or two and is then at a loss.

Very few people are directly involved with nature today other than those who farm, and even their numbers are dwindling by the hour. The great mass of mankind is city-bound by preference or necessity, and the great outdoors is used for weekend recreation, then forgotten until the next foray. Few men or women actively seek to understand and commune with it. The day of the great naturalist-writers such as John Burroughs is long past and even the fine works of such latter-day disciples as Loren Eisely and Rachel Carson have been mostly forgotten. The closest contact most urbanites have with environmental issues is the infrequent arrival of a letter from the Sierra Club, Nature Conservancy or Audubon Society soliciting contributions. As Americans have distanced themselves from the land and all that is a part of it, they have distanced themselves from their literal roots. One cannot help wonder what kind of correlation there is between the growing incidence of psychological problems among our contemporaries and this distancing.

We are, as Gibbons so well knew, surrounded by edible weeds. The word "weed" has pejorative connotations, which is unfortunate because many of these plants are quite tasty as well as being nutritious. He who knows his wild plants is not at the mercy of the wolf of starvation. And he who does not bother to learn something about them is denying himself a great deal of fascinating information and much beauty as well as a full stomach in a pinch.

What are the wild plants the would-be survivor can depend on when roughing it? One might as well ask how many raindrops make a shower. There are that many. No matter where one finds himself on this globe, whether it be on wafty mountain tops or in desiccated desert wastes, in a temperate zone, a subtropic latitude or the tropics, he will find good, wild edibles everywhere--if he knows where and how to look and how to prepare the bounty he has found. The multitude of wild edibles generally available in this country is everyone's bounty, our natural heritage. Enjoy them as a special treat in "good times." Depend upon them when things get ugly.

Before discussing some of the more common wild edibles, I refer the interested reader to two works, one already a classic in the field, the other much less well known but offering a unique and practical perspective. Euell Gibbons' *Stalking The Wild Asparagus* is a deservedly popular classic in the field of wild plants. Barrie Kavasch's *Native Harvests*, although focused specifically on recipes and botanicals of the American Indians, is also a good starting point for anyone interested in the value of foraging and gathering. The native Americans knew what was edible, what tasted good and how to prepare it simply and appealingly. We can do no better than to follow their lead.

Anyone who has an interest in learning more about wild edibles should get an illustrated book on wild plants and flowers and learn to recognize some of the plants that I am now going to mention. This will be a short study. I can do no more in reasonable space than give you an idea of the good things which have been, as often as not, at your very feet, which you may well have been scuffing about unknowingly or, quite likely, with the disdain most folks feel when in the company of plain old "weeds."

What better comestible to begin with than the lowly

and much-maligned dandelion. Here is a botanical that deserves much better than its common reputation, one that can feed us richly in a number of ways. The name, interestingly enough, comes from the Old French *dent de lion* and means tooth of the lion after the outline of the leaves. And it is the leaves we are most concerned with, especially the new ones which are most succulent. Pick these leaves young, before the plants bloom, for the freshest, tenderest taste. After-bloom leaves are quite edible as well but you may find a slightly bitter taste to them by then. If so, blanch and pour off the water, then reboil and cook them up like spinach. To make a dandelion salad, braze some young leaves and then sprinkle with oil and vinegar.

The deep yellow blooms of the dandelion are an excellent source of vitamins C and A. Eat enough of them raw and you will never have to worry about scurvy. Or make "dandelion wine" from them. Yes, there really is such a potion. What is more, the dried and baked roots of this botanical can be used as a coffee substitute, as can chicory root. Even today the Chinese still use the dandelion as a tonic, digestive aid and mild laxative. All things considered, the dandelion is a versatile performer.

The young, blanched leaves of the wild chicory, which I just mentioned in passing, and which grows prolifically in my part of Wisconsin and in many other parts of the country, are quite edible. So are the leaves of lamb's-quarters (pigweed) whose young shoots can be prepared like spinach or boiled with meat. The plentiful blackish-brown seeds are also valuable and can be crushed into a flour, as can the seeds of wild amaranth.

Other usually available botanicals with flavorful leaves are common plantain, purslane and sheep sorrel. One of the earliest wild plants to green up in my part of the Midwest is wild mustard. It has a pleasant taste raw and is edible throughout its season, although best before bloom, as are most botanicals.

Actually, less than one percent of all wild plants are truly toxic, and of the toxic ones, only a few are fatal. I would be cautious, nevertheless, in trying new specimens. Nibble lightly at first at something new. You may, unlike your neighbor, have an allergic reaction to a specific species you have not sampled before. Nibbling lightly at new things is not bad advice for the practice of life in general. I hope that doesn't sound too much like officious philosophizing from a doddering, old Polonius. The post-earth-change survivor will be called upon to sample many new things in his/her new world. It would seem advisable to experiment lightly in all things before going "whole hog" and suffering painful or fatal results.

In desperate times, especially in early spring when supplies of almost everything edible have been consumed, the succulent roots of most common field grasses can be harvested. Some are surprisingly tasty, even those of "quack grass" (couch grass), which is the only praise I can give this ubiquitous pest. Quack grass always serves to remind me that something positive can be found to be said about anything.

There are literally hundreds of edible botanicals living and thriving in and about the average one-acre, uncultivated field, whether that field is in Maine or Florida, Wisconsin or Alabama, Oregon or Texas. Many of these wild botanicals have a very wide field of distribution. They are adaptive, tough customers having survived tens of thousands of millennia on a variety of soils under often extreme conditions. And yet many of them can be found at once in all of the above-mentioned states and many adjoining ones.

Three rather ubiquitous botanicals that have a lot to offer are the common day lily, the Jerusalem artichoke and the common milkweed. To be perfectly accurate, the day lily, *Hemerocallis fulva*, is not a wild botanical but a domesticated one that has naturalized itself plentifully across much of the American countryside and is now a valuable food source. The day lily has, in fact, come full circle, from a wild ancestral state through domestication in the Orient and Europe, returning today, in many places, to a "wild," unfettered procreation. Let us hope the future evolutionary path of *Homo sapiens* will be different, although some evidence suggests man's past may well have taken a similar track. Whatever the case, let's not begrudge the bounty waiting for us along many a roadside and in many a field, especially if the time comes when a supermarket is only a memory.

In spring, the inner portions of the young, sprouting stalks of the day lily can be used in a salad or cooked like asparagus. Later in the season, the orange buds and flowers can be picked and dried for future use. They are, however, a gourmet's treat when lightly fried in butter or cooking oil. The taste is like *Agaricus campestris*, the mushroom species commercially most available. In other words, if you like deep-fried mushrooms, you will enjoy this treat immensely.

The greatest gift the day lily has to offer us does not come from above ground but from below it--the tubers. These tubers, which average about an inch long by half an inch wide, are an abundant and dependable food source at any time of year as long as the ground is not so frozen that they are inaccessible. These little morsels, washed and boiled in saltwater, taste a bit like sweet corn. Choose young, whitish tubers for your culinary experiments. The older tubers are soft and somewhat shrivelled and best left where you found them. The young, uncooked tubers, firm and sweet, make a fine, nut-flavored snack or an appealing addition to any salad of wild greens.

The second botanical of our exceptionally diverse but nutritious triumvirate is the common milkweed (*Asclepias syriaca*), which can be found in its later stages of growth waving its perfumed, purplish umbrels in the wind from Canada to northern Florida and across most of the Middle West and part of the far West. There are at least four parts of this versatile plant that are edible and can be prepared in a number of ways. But proper preparation is the key here, otherwise the results can be disappointing.

The young sprouts of the common milkweed can be eaten like asparagus. Young leaves make a passable spinach. The unopened flower buds can be eaten like broccoli. The blooming umbrels can be floured and deep-fried. And last but hardly least, young pods can be cooked like okra. But note: before any of these parts can be utilized in our outback cookery, they must be boiled briefly several times if our wilderness chef wishes to avoid the innate, lingering bitterness that permeates the whole plant.

Here's how you do it. Drop the cuttings you have chosen into boiling water. Boil for about a minute. Then remove the cuttings, drain and throw away the boiled water. Repeat this step three or four times. Then boil for ten minutes, season and enjoy.

If you plan to deep-fry the blooming umbrels, follow the previously outlined procedure except forego the last boiling. Instead, flour and season the umbrels and drop them into boiling oil and fry for a minute or two. Now you have a taste treat that you can proudly share or, if you are alone, savor yourself while wistfully wishing others were present to recognize your culinary genius. The final product is more than simply palatable and well justifies the small expenditure of energy.

The third member of our culinary triumvirate also supplies us with edible tubers, tubers which are, in my opinion, the rival of any standard potatoes anywhere. This is the Jerusalem artichoke or girasol (*Helianthus tuberosus*). Its common name is misleading because this superhardy botanical has nothing to do with Jerusalem and is not related in any way to the French artichoke with which we are all familiar. It should more properly be called the Indian potato but, unfortunately, the groundnut (*Apios americana*) has already usurped that position.

The Jerusalem artichoke is a member of the sunflower family that can make even bad cookery taste good. The sunflower family is a very large one with a lot of look-alikes. Therefore, it is wise to get a good field guide and track down this potato mini-mine. Once you've found one, you're likely to find many more, because through seeding and tuber expansion, the Jerusalem artichoke spreads rapidly. This is a boon to the survivalist who might seriously consider cultivating a few wild specimens into a productive patch.

Another wild plant with an edible tuber, and much more to offer, is the cattail. The American Indians, as well as many of the early settlers who lived in areas where lakes, rivers and marshes existed, knew the bounty of the cattail and used it throughout the seasons as a source of nourishment and fiber. Most people have no problem recognizing these tall spear-like plants topped often later in the season by rigid, brown flower stalks. As a child I fantasized using them as torches which is, indeed, a possibility if the stalks are allowed to dry thoroughly and are then dipped in kerosene. Here, however, we will concentrate upon the cattail's culinary uses, which are considerable and upon which we can depend in times of need.

About the only parts of the cattail that are not edible at some stage of growth are the leaves and the outer shell of the stalk. The leaves, however, can be used for weaving and thatching anything from baskets to hogans. Late in the season, even in midwinter, the seed heads, which have matured and produced fluffy, white heads, can be harvested and used for stuffing, fire-tinder or insulation, much like the seed pods of the mature milkweed.

In the spring, the young sprouts close to the underground (and often underwater) rhizomes are available to us when not much else in Mother Nature is. Peel away the outer shell, then eat them raw. Or cut them up and boil them and season them as you will. The taste may remind you of cucumbers although the texture is firm. You will find that from fall to spring the cattail rhizomes are at their peak and make, like girasols, a good potato substitute. The American Indians also dried them and made flour from them, thus increasing their versatility.

During the summer the cattails bloom and flower. These flowers have two distinct sections--the pollen-bearing male flower-spears at the top of the stalk and the firmer and more swollen seed-producing female flowers below (the part that looks like a torch-end). And here is a statistic I find fascinating. The flower heads of an acre of cattails will produce two to three times as much flour as an acre of wheat. This flour, which is really the plant's pollen, is very protein-rich. It can be used separately or added to other natural grains and baked up into patty bread or cakes. To harvest it, shake the cattail heads into a sack or bag. Keep this flour-pollen dry until it is used.

In early summer before the "tails" have had a chance to flower (flour), the developing flower heads can be harvested just as they turn from green to yellow. Peel the husk, boil and eat just as you would corn on the cob or a hot dog without bun.

There are many other wild sources of flour--the arrowhead plant, green amaranth, the bulrush, purslane, dock, shepherd's purse and lamb's-quarters (pigweed) among them. Once the plant is recognized and the season of the year is right--all one needs is a bowl and pestle to go to work. And it is work, sometimes hard work to grind small seeds the old way. But when one is without choice, and hungry, it is surprising how pleased and satisfied a wild flour muffin or pancake can leave us. The hard work is soon forgotten after a good night's sleep on a full stomach.

Before we move on in our journey through the natural landscape studying what, other than wild plants, might sustain us when former channels of manufactured foodstuffs have ceased to exist, I would like to focus briefly on two additional plant sources, Queen Ann's Lace and young ferns. In my part of the Midwest, the wild carrot (Queen Ann's Lace) seems to grow everywhere, especially in open, uncultivated fields. It is only in the last century that our domesticated carrot as we know it was bred from this wild forebear. Although the raw root of the wild carrot is stringy and tough, it can be cut up into small pieces and boiled until tender. Now it is transformed and has become quite table-worthy. The pleasantly pungent broth that remains can be used for a soup base.

One of the first signs of early spring in many regions of the country is the appearance of fern fiddleheads. What is a "fiddlehead"? It is the spirally coiled young fronds of any number of fern species, also called "crosiers." Orientals and New Zealanders have long appreciated the delectable taste of fiddleheads, but this gourmet's delight is almost completely unknown in the United States where fern fiddleheads are quite common, particularly in the northern and southeastern states. Three of the larger ferns that produce good-sized crosiers are the Bracken (*Pteridium*) fern, the Ostrich fern (*Pteretis nodulosa*) and the Cinnamon fern (*Osmunda cinnamomea*). Pick some when they have sprouted from 2 to 9 inches above their crowns, and leave some so that the plant can regenerate itself. Then boil your stolen booty like asparagus, steam, sautee it with butter or steep it in a fine cream sauce. You will find these fiddleheads are fine fare all around, particularly with toast or as an additional course with meat and soup. If you wish to freeze them, blanch for several minutes, then quick-freeze. Later they may be unthawed at your discretion, cooked for 8 to 10 minutes, eaten appreciatively, and the memory savored for the rest of the day.

In the North, fiddleheads appear in April and May at a time when the forager may be searching desperately for something green and edible. The fern family, as ancient as 400 million or more years old, almost forgotten and vastly underappreciated by most modern food gathers (although represented by 10,000 to 12,000 species), has been waiting patiently all the while to serve man when needed.

Picking Mushrooms

A word or two here on gathering and eating wild mushrooms is not out of place. The *idea* of picking mushrooms is romantic. The reality can be much different.

It is probably fortunate that most people do not actualize their impulse to haphazardly gather mushrooms more than they do, because the gathering and eating of fungi is dangerous business. There are really only two categories of mushroom pickers--novices and experts. Thousands of novices end up in hospitals every year. Some die. Experts are very careful and here's why.

I have gathered and eaten cooked, wild mushrooms for over 25 years. I have an extensive library of books on fungi, which I have, for identification purposes, much used. Many of the book spines and page margins are stained with smudges of spore prints and field dirt. I have a microscope I almost invariably use to check spore prints--always in an attempt to verify what I have or think I have. With fungi a new experience is always right around the next tree trunk. I am continually discovering what I don't know, often in contradistinction to what I thought I knew.

Even as careful as I have been, I have been poisoned twice. Once a friend did the honors. The other time I poisoned myself. The last poisoning, interestingly enough, came from a species that the field guides all stated was edible. I had, I suppose, an allergic reaction to this particular species. This is, believe me, something that can happen to any one of us each time we ingest a foodstuff with which we (and our body) are not familiar and which, we soon find, our particular system cannot tolerate. With wild mushrooms, one man's gourmet treat can become another man's nightmare. The problem some people have with strawberries is a well known example.

If you insist on gathering mushrooms, have a very knowledgeable person (an expert) teach you about some of the more common edible species. Then be very cautious. To begin with, eat only a small, cooked portion of a new species. No more than a square centimeter or two of one single cap. Then wait six hours to see if you happen to react adversely. Take spore prints as you become more interested in gathering and wish to widen your knowledge of new edible species. Learn to use the color of the spore print as an identification sign. Buy a good microscope and use the shape and size of spores to further indicate to you what species you have found.

The Great Lakes area of the United States is one of the richest places in the world for sheer numbers of fungi species and diversity of fungi genera. It also has some of the world's most toxic species such as *Amanita phalloides, Amanita verna, Amanita virosa* ("Destroying Angel") and some of the *Galerina*. Many of these species are large and strikingly beautiful. They look intensely sumptuous and succulent--and they will kill you slowly and painfully within five or six days, after your liver and kidneys have failed, after convulsions and ultimate heart failure. I think you'll agree this is a very painful way to exit the world.

If I have failed to dissuade you, if you are bold and insist on plunging into this fascinating field of research, begin by collecting a few species that are relatively easy to recognize--such as the true morels (e.g. *Morchella esculenta, Morchella deliciosa, Morchella angusticeps)*, *Pleurotus ostreatus*, which grows like overlapping oysters on old wood, *Armilleria mellea* (the "honey" mushroom), puffballs (but beware of mistaking *Scleroderma* for small ones) and perhaps members of the *Boletus* genus, the ones which do not turn bluish or reddish-blue underneath and do not have a variegated reddish-green cap. And always remember, even a popular and much picked genus like *Morchella*, which is usually considered safe, has its dangerous, poisonous look-alikes. These are known as false morels and include species of *Gyromitra* which can be fatal. And never put any stock in the many old wives' tales which purportedly tell how to distinguish a mushroom from a toadstool (the words are synonymous) and a poisonous fungus from an edible one. For example, it is said that a piece of silver in a boiling pot of mushrooms will turn black if the mushrooms are poisonous. Tommyrot. The only thing you can be sure of is that the silver is wet.

The survivor of earth changes who finds himself in the field had best leave the fungi alone. There are usually many good, wild botanicals around that will feed him sufficiently, sometimes royally. He need not risk his life ordinarily on dubious fare when surer, more friendly members of the natural world abound. I stated earlier that less than one percent of wild plants are toxic. Although I have not seen any studies which indicate what relative percentage of fungi are toxic to some degree or another, I can assure you it would be much higher. Why not avoid Russian roulette when it is your life that is at stake?

The trusted friend who poisoned me with his *Russula* soup was quite sure of what he had. I took his word for it. This was a huge mistake. With fungi you take only your own word--no one else's--and that sometimes with trepidation. At any rate, I found myself flat on my back in a tent in the northern woods in the middle of the night. I was unable to breath for about three minutes. For those minutes I was sure I was going to die. But I promised myself that, if I lived, I would never, ever again be so foolish. I would eat no mushrooms unless I had carefully inspected them myself, until I had made my own tests. And I have kept my word--and am still around to tell about it.

Gathering Nuts, Fruits and Berries

There is nothing quite as delectable as "found" fruit and berries. These are the wild apples, plums, cherries, persimmons, paw paws, mulberries, walnuts, hickory nuts, butternuts, hazelnuts, strawberries, blackberries, dewberries, raspberries, gooseberries, currants and all their woodland cousins which are espied and gathered either by accident or plan. Today it is good, leisure-fun to harvest these often neglected nuggets. Tomorrow it may become a necessity.

The woods and meadows of rural America still contain an abundance of all of the above-named edibles. We are particularly blessed with a large array of wild nut trees. Wild nuts of all kinds were once an Indian and early settler staple. Flour can be made from any of the nuts of the edible species, and this includes both white oak and red oak. The kernels of white oak nuts (acorns) are the sweetest, but red oak nuts can also be expropriated for emergency cookery as long as they are blanched several times to remove the tannic acid as much as possible. Even white oak nuts benefit from one or more blanchings. The American Indian highly valued oil pressed or boiled from acorns as well as flour made from them. Nut kernels and nut flour could be stored and kept for extended periods of time, which was advantageous when these products were compared to more perishable foodstuffs.

Nuts are high in protein. They can become a dietary replacement for the protein many of us gain, somewhat inadvisably, from red meats. It is a fact that most American vegetarians who maintain a well-rounded intake of fruits, vegetables and nuts live an average of five to six years longer than their meat-eating countrymen. Whether this is due to the lower cholesterol levels of such fare, or to other causes such as the avoidance of meat-borne bacteria and chemical and antibiotic additives, is hard to say. The longevity increase could be caused by a combination of such factors as well as factors not yet completely understood. Lifestyle may well play a large part. The typical vegetarian does not seem as driven or stressed out as is his meat-eating counterpart. General philosophy of life should not be discounted from any equation which tries to explain the longevity disparity between the two groups. Whatever the cause, a truism remains which is pertinent to the lot of the earth-change survivor: You do not have to have meat in your diet to be healthy, strong and full of energy. And these characteristics, needless to say, are at a premium when there is much work to be done in circumstances which are far from ideal.

One final word on gathering apples, nuts and berries. I have often noticed the many unpicked fruit trees within city limits as well as in the countryside. The amount of wasted fruit is appalling. The reasons for this abandonment and waste, I have concluded, are several. First, we are a well-fed nation too used to squandering much of our bounty. We take too much for granted in all things. Secondly, people avoid fruit that has blemishes, and much of the fruit from these unsprayed trees is slightly blemished in one way or another. The public has been trained by the advertising arm of the commercial fruit industry to believe that a fruit with a spot on it is a bad fruit. This is basically balderdash. For example, the marks left on an apple by scab or curculio activity in no way damage the quality of the interior flesh. Peel the blems away if you must, although this is not necessary, and in doing so, you loose the substantial vitamin content of the skin along with its fiber-value. Thirdly, it would appear many of us are too lazy to harvest the abundant fruits that Mother Nature created in our immediate vicinity. The old adage, waste not, want not, seems applicable. Modern man wastes much. In the future he may want much. In earth-change times, the lazy man cannot expect others to feed him. Should he persist in his folly and wait for the apple, so to speak, to fall into his mouth, he will pass sentence on himself. The verdict: starvation.

Hunting

The question of whether it is advisable to hunt for game with firearms or other mechanisms is a difficult one. Under extreme conditions where starvation is imminent, a

118

strong argument can be made that it is justified. There still remains the question of whether it is a moral act consistent with the cosmic law that all living things (and everything is alive) are sacred and to be cherished and protected.* This law applies particularly to higher life forms which have an active intelligence, and this would include, of course, the animal forms most usually hunted. Plants are also alive and intimately related to everything else in creation, just as we humans are, although we often forget. For higher life forms such as ourselves, there exists an operational dispensation to harvest these plants and lower life forms for sustenance.

Many extraterrestrial cultures, if we are to believe some of the humans who claim to have had contact with them (and I do believe *some* of them), refrain from using animal forms as foodstuff.   They choose to live a vegetarian existence, in deference to greater cosmic law. Some in fact use only, or mainly, foodstuffs manufactured out of raw chemicals, thus avoiding the destruction of any living form other than the most unelaborated and least complex. An atom is, after all, an alive and active bundle of energy and mass whether it is found in a stone or in the heart of a man.

It remains primarily up to each individual as to what limits he or she imposes upon himself or herself in all things.   Some will choose not to hunt no matter how rigorous the conditions, no matter how hungry they become. They should not, under any circumstances, be faulted for this.   They have an innate right to their choice backed by cosmic law. Others will choose to hunt only

---

*As Thomas Banyacya, interpreter of the Coyote Clan for the Hopi elders, has said, "All things are alive and interrelated and breathe from the same center of creation."

119

under conditions of extreme hardship.

For those who do choose to hunt, an adequate supply of ammunition becomes an imperative. It should always be kept in mind by the confirmed hunter that if conditions remain harsh, and the usual channels of supply fail, then sooner or later his ammunition will run out and recourse to other methods of taking game will become necessary. It is possible to use bow and arrow, crossbow, slingshot, blowgun, snare, pit, trap and other devices for this purpose. I will not go into the niceties of how to manufacture these devices. My experience is limited. Most, however, if desired, can be purchased now and stored away for future use. And there are many written works available which describe how to manufacture these mechanisms and how to use them.

There is another large question which arises about taking game during a period of massive, worldwide earth changes. This is the question of species conservation. We are familiar with the stories of the buffalo and passenger pigeon which were ruthlessly hunted; in the former case, almost to extinction, in the latter case, to complete extinction. Even in the somewhat protected environment of today, where hunting regulations abound, certain large animal species have become rare. Many, such as the Dall sheep and Kodiak bear, never existed in great numbers and, then as now, only in specific, limited habitats. There is a great danger in this world so heavily populated with humanity that if unrestrained hunting should become common, because of earth changes, many marginal species will be quickly wiped out. Desperation often is its own worst enemy. What good is it to overharvest today when tomorrow our overharvesting will contribute to our going hungry? This applies also to the gathering of flora as well. The Amerindians were (and still are) careful to take only what they needed and to always leave some plants untouched. These remained to reproduce and flourish for a distant day when they would be much appreciated.

Fishing

Except for porpoises and whales, which are quite evolved and relatively intelligent, I can see no impelling reason to have qualms about harvesting fish in reasonable quantities for foodstuff on this planet. Saltwater fish are high in protein and vitamins A and D. Almost all fish are generally nutritious. And besides, they taste good when prepared either by frying, baking or broiling. They can also be easily dried, as Amerindians well knew.

Almost all species of fresh and saltwater fish are edible, and most species are safe to consume, although cases of *ciguatera* poisoning sometimes occur in the Caribbean and the Central and South Pacific.*

It does not usually take great knowledge or finesse to catch fish. Nor does one have to have fancy, specialized equipment. I do have a weakness for such equipment and have fished widely in both fresh and saltwater, but I know better. Some good hooks, a rod, a hundred yards or so of good nylon or monofilament line and a simple reel will suffice under most conditions. As a matter of fact, any six

---

*Certain puffer fish, which are found in saltwater, are notoriously toxic. There were reports several decades ago that the CIA had experimented with puffer fish toxins.

to eight-foot piece of bamboo or tree limb with line tied directly to one end will usually work effectively, as Isaak Walton and Dame Juliana Berners well knew. They also appreciated the advantages of the simple worm as bait and the value of earth-grubs as well. Many people the world over use only the hand line to catch all the fish they need. I had this ably demonstrated to me in the 60s while fishing the estuary at San Blas, Mexico by a local guide, Abalone Ordaz. Fishing a hand line is exactly what it sounds like, simply a line, hook and bait either trolled from a boat or thrown by hand and retrieved hand over hand from a stationary boat or while wading or shore-bound.

Most areas of North America have streams, rivers, lakes or ponds nearby. Some have an abundance of fresh water. In times of crisis and hunger, fish can become a welcome addition to the diet. With many early native Americans, such as the Tlingit of the coastal areas of southern Alaska and northern British Columbia, fish became a staple food resource. To ignore this resource in needy, hungry times is to court extreme privation when "plenty" is at hand.

Under the worst conditions, the would-be survivor must become a jack-of-all-trades. He must learn to be a forager, fisherman and, if he chooses, hunter. By thus adapting himself, he insures the survival of his bodily self and those around him who depend on him. And while in the act of preserving himself physically, it is quite likely he will be reminded sooner or later, even if his former "civilized" self has somehow made him forget, that everything in this natural world is intimately related to everything else. It is within that interdependence that he has his unique being, and it will most likely occur to him sometime that whatever satisfaction he finds, whatever nobility he discovers in himself or the actions of those about him, is anchored within those interconnections. To always insist on going it alone is not only a prescription for loneliness but a denial of the complex and interwoven matrix of life that gives us our being and of which we are a small, though vital, part.

11

Maintaining an Adequate Defense

Crimes of violence, as we are all aware, are momentarily rampant and increasing statistically year by year. We live in a world whose roots are violent, on a continent whose history is violent, in a culture today that often celebrates violence. Now may well be the most violent period in our national history, although adequate statistics are not available to indisputably confirm such a conclusion.

What statistics are at hand paint a dangerous, depressing picture of life in America. For example, in 1991 a total of 38,300 people died of gunshot wounds, almost as many as died in automobile accidents. Many of these deaths were accidents, to be sure. Some suicides. But according to the FBI's *Uniform Crime Reports* (1992), there were 22,540 murders reported for the year. Of these, 15,377 involved firearms, 12,489 involved handguns.   There were 9.3 murders for each 100,000 citizens, and the average citizen stood about one chance in 20 of being a victim of some kind of felony.

Fear has come to be a silent, debilitating presence that accompanies almost everyone everywhere.   As Cornel West recently observed in *Newsweek*, "This fear now permeates much of America--fear of violent attack or vicious assault, fear of indecent exposure or malicious insult.   Out of the 80s came a new kind of civic terrorism--physical and psychic--that haunts the public streets and private minds of America."

We are certainly not the only violent culture on the face of the earth.   It is true that Europe and Japan still have a much lower incidence of crimes directed against the person when compared to the United States.   If we combine the murder rates of both geographical areas, for example, the total is still minuscule compared to that found in the U.S.   Yet the incidence of violent crime is rapidly increasing in these two areas of the world.   And since the breakup of the former Soviet Union, crime in the CIS (Confederation of Independent States) has skyrocketed. Moscow, once a relatively safe place to walk the streets, has now joined the ranks of New York City, Chicago, Los Angeles, Rio de Janeiro, London and the majority of other major Western cities where the stroller had best be on guard if he values his life and possessions.   Throughout the CIS unorganized street gangs and the Russian mafiosi with their new army of *boyeviks* (mafia soldiers) are vying to control everything from street commerce to high finance.

There are few places under the sun where there are fewer violent crimes committed against individuals and society at large than there were a few decades (or few years) ago. Of course, much of the world has always been relatively dangerous, but never in recent history has the individual been as exposed to personal, physical attack from other human beings as he/she is today.

What are the causes of this worldwide situation? It is quite obviously not a simple problem with simple answers. The factors involved are multiple, staggering in their implications, beyond, it would seem, the ability of sociologists and psychologists to define them or politicians and police departments to contain them. There has not been, especially in the Western World, a nonviolent breakdown of such scale in traditional values since the Renaissance, and a violent breakdown of such magnitude since the gradual collapse of the Roman Empire during the 3rd, 4th and 5th centuries. As I wrote in *When Men Are Gods*, a culture without direction, without guiding values, whether these are traditional or new-found, is a culture headed for the precipice. Whether it plunges over or not depends very much on how quickly and well (if at all) it is able to redefine itself.

The 20th century has seen a terrifying erosion of traditional religious values and other customs and mores. Such alternatives as "situational morality," humanistic existentialism or the latest cult fashion are not the moral underpinnings from which a smoothly functioning culture, and a nonviolent one, stands and endures. As of late, much of popular culture produced in the West ridicules, parodies and directly attacks ideas of order and harmony. How can the average citizen, whether he lives in Rome, Tokyo, New York City or elsewhere, have much confidence in politicians and statesmen when he sees uncovered for him daily in the mass media their greedy, corrupted deeds? Respect for the individual, the family and the social institution, which gradually rose from the Renaissance through the 19th century, has appreciably diminished of late in the last decades of the 20th century. And this has happened at a time when phony democracy (as compared to the real thing, which is rare) has unwittingly uncovered more and more the vast inequality in wages and lifestyle between the more-than-comfortable and the struggling poor. The controlled mass media, which is so good most of the time at manipulating public attitudes, has, by the very mechanism of its own machinery, created a tiger which threatens to devour it and all who are caught within the web of its influence.

Expectations are an irresistible force not easily contained. People once insular and uneducated about local and international affairs, are now haphazardly but steadily exposed to realities which they scarcely would have dreamed of several decades ago but which they are little prepared to understand. Even in its most bland and orchestrated verion, this "news" has awakened them. They now often feel that life--which includes their government and the institutions it represents--has cheated them or, at best, given them less than is possible or less than they have come to expect is rightfully theirs. The public generally is unsettled and angered by the inequality it perceives in the distribution of the world's wealth. Many have become blatant scofflaws (e.g. the Crips and Bloods) or quiet scofflaws (e.g. the BCCI bankers, the Michael Milkens and Ivan Boeskys). It is increasingly common to find those who are skeptical of everything or believe in nothing--unless it is having their own way. Such, in a nutshell, is how we have become so subjective, so twisted inward, so dangerous to those about us, at a time when the world desperately needs clear, objective thinking, true democracy, a sharing of wealth and resources and an abiding peace on earth which will allow mankind to reach its true, almost limitless, potential.

What does all this have to do with massive earth changes? A great deal. Massive earth changes unleash the Four Horsemen of the Apocalypse. Your can read that either literally or metaphorically, as is your persuasion. But the reality remains constant: Massive earth changes unleash war, famine, disease and death. The greater the changes, the greater the amount of random social violence we can expect, especially at the height of each great change with a diminishing intensity relatively proportionate to the time removed from the cataclysm(s) whatever it (they) might be. The individual mortal will be sorely vulnerable to those without scruples or compassion. Even small groups of men and women who have banded together and are striving to survive peacefully will be profoundly challenged from time to time. Armageddon, massive earth changes, or both at once, may well lead us into a new Dark Age. To be unprepared may result in our becoming a sacrificial lamb to the marauders of night and day.

New Age spokesman Shawn Atlanti has said, "The day of the armed cutthroat is over. We aren't going to have a world like that." And I heartily agree. Those who think that all they have to do to survive is stock enough .308 or 30-06 ammunition are mistaken. And, I might add, greatly unprepared for the mental and physical demands that will be made upon them. But you can be sure some of this type will be on the move. And many of them will believe that force will prevail--their force. Most will shortly die by the violence they live by. Until that time comes, the would-be survivor had best be prepared to deal with them.

One of the more foolish notions, which I have repeatedly cautioned against, is the idea that the remnants of any remaining government will be there to protect us. Do not count on it and take, if you will, the Los Angeles earthquake experience of January, 1994, as an object lesson. As quakes are measured, this one (6.6 Richter scale) was not a large one, and yet it killed 53 or more human beings and did an estimated 30 billion dollars worth of damage. It also brought governmental services personnel to their knees. "All the normal routes have broken down--sanitation, purified water, adequate nutrition," said Mary Copeland, wellness coordinator at Pepperdine University in a recent *Milwaukee Sentinel* article. "It's like losing your civilization. You look at those tent cities and have to realize that's what is going on. Their world has been reduced to ground zero-- literally." If this is the aftermath of a minor earth change, what can we expect from changes immensely greater and more far ranging?

If remnants of federal, state and local governments do survive, they will most likely be thoroughly overwhelmed and, in most cases, unable to respond. Law enforcement agencies, if they still exist, will be helplessly outmanned while, at the same time, completely overloaded with demand. If it is possible to preserve order and peace by lending a hand to one of these organizations, and this is your wish, by all means do so. Equitable order, that is. Fair peace. If, however, you find these official organs nonexistent, totally ineffective or corrupt beyond salvage, you had best make plans to protect yourself and those who depend upon you.

How do you do that? Probably the best course of

action is to join ranks with a group of friends or like-minded new acquaintances who have similar ideas of peaceful survival (see chapter eight, "The Importance of Community"). In urban areas, where gangs are likely to prowl, this is especially necessary. Here we are talking about forming neighborhood protection organizations. Certain individuals who seem competent to act as standby policemen should be appointed. It is most probable that they will have to be armed or at least have immediate access to protective firearms. These individuals, it goes without saying, must be well-adjusted, calm, cool-headed people capable of the great responsibility that policing their fellows entails. They must also be cautioned to respond to strangers in a completely equitable, friendly manner.

I do not like advocating the possession or use of firearms. I hesitate to do it, but I am also realistic. A totally unarmed group of well-meaning people are, in the opinion of a certain kind of humanity, tender meat waiting for the slaughter. It isn't necessary to flaunt the defensive possession of firearms. In fact, it could be a gross mistake, attracting the attention of those who are violence-prone, mentally unstable or simply thieves. I suggest keeping all weapons undercover but readily available for those moments when they are needed. At those moments, an alarm can be sounded, bringing the larger, well-armed group quickly together for mutual defense.

As I have indicated earlier, it is the urban survivors who are most vulnerable to human predation and victimization of one sort or another. If you are an urban survivor, get out into the countryside if possible; the less populated the area, the better. Hook up with like-thinking individuals. Find, if possible, a setting which can be farmed effectively and defended if need be.   Erect adequate shelter. Let each man or woman perform the work they are best at. Let each work according to his/her own capacity.* Let everyone pitch in when the situation calls for it. Elect certain individuals as peace-keepers, as your policemen, but teach everyone how to defend themselves, even with firearms if necessary. Have a bell or other loud alarm that can be heard from a distance readily available so that the "group" can be rapidly called together when needed.   And always remember to use force defensively and only as much force as is absolutely necessary--and not a mite more.

It is a timeworn biblical proverb that, "He who lives by the sword shall die by the sword." It is also utterly true.

If the intinerant lazy or troublesome happen along and wish to join your party for their own selfish reasons, give them a little food, if you have some to spare, be firm with them and tell them the ship is full. Thank them for their offer and send them on their way.

The same advice applies to the malingerer who is already a part of the group. If he or she is not willing to pull his or her own weight, wish them well and send them off. Be satisfied that you have been compassionate and done your Christian duty. A rogue elephant, whether lazy or not, can easily destroy both the village and its occupants in short order. It is wiser to face up to such a problem early on, than to vacillate and postpone the inevitable until great damage has been done.

With luck, some preparation and much firmness of

---

*Ideas reminiscent of Jeremy Bentham and his sometimes copycat, Karl Marx, but without the bureaucratic leanings and general mean-spiritedness inherent in the ideas of the latter.

will, the survivors of massive earth changes will have a fighting chance to begin a new life. Out of the rubble that surrounds them, slowly but surely, a new community can be built. If it will endure, it must dedicate itself to peace on earth and the continuing enlightenment of each individual member, no matter how difficult the task or how dark the present moment may seem.

12

Maintaining the Rudiments of Civilization

It is interesting to speculate on what the future of the Western World might have been had not the great library at Alexandria been destroyed several times, the last time most thoroughly sometime between 391 and 646 A.D.* It is also interesting to speculate what thoughts crossed the mind of that crisp prose writer, Julius Caesar, an educated warrior who valued learning, when he was told that 40,000 or more of the library's books had been destroyed during his defense of the city in 47 B.C. The Alexandrian library was, in its long history, the greatest acknowledged repository of the wisdom of the ancient Near East, watched over and maintained at various times by some of the greatest scholars of the day--Zenodotus of Ephesus, the poet Callimachus, Aristophanes of Byzantium, Aristarchus

---

*There is no agreement as to when the library was finally destroyed.

of Samothrace and, perhaps most notably, the wise and beautiful Hypatia, who was most brutally murdered by her jealous male competitors.

After the library's fall and the final sacking of Rome, Western civilization was no doubt greatly impoverished and, like a young delinquent without proper foundation and guidance, slipped rapidly into a nonintellectual miasma from which it was only gradually able to raise itself many centuries later.

It may well be that the libraries of Byzantium, Rome and the Arab world preserved much of the ancient wisdom, and that the monasteries of Tibet and other hidden crannies of the East still hold treasures of lost wisdom. It is also probably true that ancient records (such as those of the legendary Hermes Trismegistus) still lie buried in Egypt and other parts of the world, such as Mexico and Central and South America. We have the Mormon tablets experience to add credence to such thinking along with rumors which have drifted through recorded history like a Shekinah-fog eluding the grasp of human hands and minds. But the truth is that, if these repositories still exist, they are known to only a silent few or remain still unfound, unearthed, biding their time until, through luck or intuition, they are upturned to the light of day.

What slender, delicate reeds of understanding that we have cultivated in the arts and sciences over the past several thousand years are precious to us. And they are vulnerable. We must protect them if we can. Even if much of the science is faulty. Even though much of this "wisdom" has often been found to be lacking and far from perfected. We must, come an Armageddon or massive earth changes, make every effort to preserve as much as possible--that we might build from whatever survives and remains, build truer and better the house of our philosophy and our science. Then the civilizations that succeed us will have the best foundation and structure that we can leave them.

There is no mistaking the fact that great civilizations of prehistory have existed on planet Earth. The ruins of Stonehenge, Silbury Hill, Baalbek, Petra, the Gobi desert, Machu Picchu, Tiahuanaco, Sacsahuaman and many others give mute testimony that even in the more recent prehistory of earth, great civilizations have existed, flowered magnificently and then mysteriously disappeared, leaving only some colossal structures of earth and stone for fleet birds to flit about and wild winds to whistle through and human minds to wonder at in their confusion. Are these the remains of civilizations destroyed by random cataclysms, periodic or cyclic massive earth changes? Perhaps the natural causes have been various. Wars may well have played a part in their depopulation. But war as the sole agent seems unlikely in all cases. Great cities once conquered, if still intact, are almost invariably inhabited by conquerors and survivors. The explanation is best looked for elsewhere.

And looking elsewhere leads us ultimately, first perhaps by intuition or tapping into our unconscious racial memory, to the concept of great natural catastrophes. Popular science, including academic science, has resisted the idea that the true geologic history of this planet could be as periodically or randomly violent as it appears to have been. Lyellian geology, the theory of uniformitarian change, appeases the troubled human spirit, promising nothing so terrible, so stark a reminder of nature's potential and often swift fury, as the astroblemes that dot the face of the earth, as the evidence that exists for prehistoric axis shifts, as the piles of arctic mammoth bones and other animals here and there attesting to a great, almost worldwide, deluge, as the evidence of the Bannock overthrust and thrusts in other parts of the world, as the tremendous foraminifera die-offs separating so many geologic ages, as the more subtle, yet compelling, large O^{18} (oxygen 18) variations found in ice core samples taken from the Greenland icecap. Yet great events did take place. There is no denying these facts. *And there is much scientific evidence of other violent earth changes in our planet's past, and simply labelling all the anomalies that exist as erratica, as potentially explainable disconformities, and dismissing them will not make them go away.* The "record of the rocks" suggests repeated changes. Great, consuming, wrenching, smothering, life-blotting changes.

It is necessary to read the works of those who are passed over today by conventional science as maverick philosophers, geologists, scientists, and sometimes as just plain self-deluded egotists, to get an idea of the substantial evidence that exists, and can be confirmed, for these historic and prehistoric cataclysms. The works of the older geologists, men such as William Buckland, William Whewell, John Woodward, Abraham Gottlob Werner, Georges Louis Leclerc (Comte de Buffon), Georges Cuvier, Charles Murchison, the Frenchmen D'Archiac and D'Orbigny, Henry Howorth and Joseph Prestwich lay the foundations for an active catastrophism. Later and present- day works by George McCready Price, Immanuel Velikovsky, Donald Patten, Luis and Walter Alvarez, Richard Muller, Daniel Whitmire, David Raup, John Sepkoski, V. Clube, Eugene Shoemaker, G. W. Wetherill,

R. Ganapathy, Claude Albritton and a host of other contemporary investigators have furthered the case for an active catastrophism which manifests itself in a variety of possible guises. All raise up for inspection either the evidence of great catastrophes during the earth's past evolution or point out the logic, including the mathematical probability, that the earth has undergone repeated and successive episodes of violent "events." I suspect that if our science survives into the near future, it will not be long before the orthodox interpretation of earth's geologic history is radically revised and within that revision will be an acknowledgment of the many natural catastrophes past and future to which earth man is heir.

Although the pressures of the moment may come to seem overwhelming, it is exceedingly important to our future as a civilized race that, should worse come to worst, every effort be made to preserve basic educational materials. By this I mean books, tapes, videos, microfilm and cassettes which contain the history of the race; that is, human learning such as it is. I am well aware that immediate considerations of subsistence may not, in the aftermath of great cataclysms, allow much time for leisurely study. Nevertheless, as soon as possible, the education of any surviving small children must be continued. This is a critical necessity. To ignore it is to court barbarism within a generation or two. Unfortunately, this may well have been the fate of several advanced civilizations in the earth's past. Certainly, if we are to give any credence to Plato's priests of Sais, it has happened at least once in recorded history, although those records have either been destroyed or lie mouldering, waiting to be found.* Whatever the case, we should never underestimate how quickly, once relieved of the trappings of culture, humankind can revert to an illiterate and unkind primitivism.

What can the lone survivor do to help insure a literate future for those he finds about him? He/she can make a special effort, if at all possible, to maintain in safekeeping books, dictionaries and other media that can later be used by juveniles and adults alike. Such planning is not fatalistic; it is not ridiculous. Quite the contrary. It is realistic and practical. A good mind hopes the best for the future but is aware of how capricious and unpredictable the happiness of the moment can be, and how on the instant a sky-change can bring disaster.

There is little hope that public educational institutions will be functioning immediately following massive earth changes. They may well have ceased to exist altogether. Once survivors have banded together into communal groups, and soon after these groups have ordered themselves and begun to shelter, feed and clothe themselves, it is time for the group to marshal its educational resources and commit itself to the continuing education of its children. As on the old frontier, so now. The need to instill the ability to read and write as well as to do simple mathematics is crucial as a socializing and civilizing influence. A teacher or teachers should be chosen. These most logically would be individuals who have had previous experience in formal education or

---

*The priests of Sais were referring to the destruction of Atlantis which may have been concurrent with, and partly the cause of, what is called the Great Deluge or Noah's flood. The primary cause(s) of either event remains uncertain and is a matter of speculation, although there is mounting evidence that both events did occur whether concurrently or not.

simply those who seem to have a talent for it.

Banding together to learn creates a sense of community. Banding is often synonymous with bonding, and many of a child's early social-bonding experiences (other than familial bonding) occur during his or her school days.

Our pioneer ancestors were well aware that learning and social pleasure could go hand in hand. The husking bees, Sunday socials and more formal Chautauguas of the past centuries are examples. Even if children are absent, which they need not be, the psychological and sociological benefits of adults getting together to sing, dance, talk and even study cannot be overestimated. Where people meet, even in adversity, there is a human need to relax and socialize. Man is a marvelously gregarious creature. When working together, as stated in Genesis, "there is nothing he cannot do."

13

Mental Firmness

In a time of great, protracted earth changes, only those who have developed true mental firmness are likely to survive. Pretenders and the self-deluded will fool no one, not even themselves, for long because stark conditions have a way of unmasking pretense. Brash thoughtlessness of all kinds will end in grief, as it always has, although maybe sooner than it sometimes has. Braggarts and would-be heroes will find people in general less willing to wait for results, unwilling because of necessity to accept hot air in place of performance. A world reduced to physical, mental and spiritual basics has its own virtues and rewards, although we have become much unused to them in these times of permissiveness and dissembling.

I hesitate to write about mental "toughness." I prefer instead to use the word "firmness" for several reasons. First, we are not talking here about thugs or wrestling. On the contrary, we are arguing that the mind must dominate the body, take absolute, premeditated control of it, if the earth-change survivor is to endure privations that the unwilling body, left to its own simple, biological devices, could not master. We need survivors who are thinkers, who are thinking all their waking hours--and using their will power, which they must internally generate, to guide this thinking.

Simple physical "toughness," brutishness of any kind, will not do. Our culture is used to confusing apples with oranges. We are as much as not encouraged to do this, and we pay a terrible price for it. The verbal combination "mental toughness" is really a subtle oxymoron, a juxtaposition of words that represent two contradictory states or impulses. Being only tough will definitely not save us in the long run, although it sometimes has short-term benefits. Thinking clearly and effectively all the time, short-term and long-term, just might.

Our culture generally indulges itself verbally and luxuriates in confusing itself, often without realizing it. This kind of behavior does not prepare us very well for the day when clear thinking and speaking will be a life and death matter. I have no doubt it is to the benefit of some to have a mentally and verbally confused populace. A nation that cannot or does not (either consciously or naturally) place a priority on straight thinking is more easily manipulated than one which takes great care to insure that words (which are symbols) clearly reflect as well as possible the reality of whatever they are intended to represent. A nation that refuses to think straight is, therefore, not going to be able to write and speak clearly and vice versa.

The present-day tendency is to undermine language, to

misuse words (e.g. when "bad" means "good"), to create verbal flummery and puffery, to mumble almost meaningless approval and disapproval noises (e.g. "It was a fantastic movie," "She is a great girl"), to expropriate words for psychological warfare (often known as "advertising"), and to hang inappropriate connotations on them, secondhand connections that the words have not had in the past. This is often done out of ignorance, sometimes out of perversity and too many times with purposive intent to deceive and mislead. As a longtime teacher of language, I am well aware that language grows and changes gradually over time as people who use it modify it. This is honest change. It is a process sensitive to the heartbeat of the people who use it, who literally make it.

But what is happening today in this culture, and generally in the Western World, is not most often honest, natural change. It is, rather, manipulation, sometimes carefully orchestrated and presented as harmless and ingenuous and spontaneously occurring when in fact it is anything but spontaneous. It is created by a small clique of opinion-setters, those who fancy themselves because of their power and influence to be great movers and shakers. And it is intended to bend and skew the straight mind, to elevate emotional response and smother logical thinking.

These mind-molders, through conscious and subliminal means, with the public's quiet, thoughtless acquiescence, have made us often see black for white, megalomaniacs as statesmen, the slightly talented as "stars," the shrewd and devious as philanthropic, the platitudinous as wise . . . . They have almost convinced us in America that real mental firmness has something to do with professional athletics. We live in a soft age that is given to self-praise and prizes its mental delusion that it is self-reliant. Remove for a few moments one single, essential public service such as electricity, which happened with the widespread blackout in New York City and the Northeast in 1965, and utter confusion results.

If any of us are to survive great future earth changes, we had better get our heads clear and straight. No matter what the cause of addleheaded thinking, it is of no use and has no place in times of crisis.

If a person is to be a survivor of natural catastrophes the *sine qua non* is a mental firmness which faces realities head on and works out logically and coolly but compassionately the best way(s) to proceed. Because our society has not lately much honored this characteristic (although it has pretended to value it), it is difficult to know who among us is capable of rising to the occasion. Certainly we must exclude from consideration most elected public officials, who are so accustomed to compromising their integrity that it is hard to believe most of them still might have a quantity of mental firmness left from which to draw. And most of the truly wealthy are too busy entertaining their desires, too softened by having their whims perpetually gratified, to have left much of a reserve for clear, selfless thinking. Regrettably, one's present standing in the community is not a very good indication either of the presence of this characteristic. Neither is one's financial status, excluding the idle rich and the hedonistic wealthy, who have already been written off generally as relatively hopeless cases. Nor is one's physical stature. Brawn and mental firmness do not necessarily have anything in common. They are not, however, mutually exclusive.

Remember those old movies? The ones where, let's

say, a plane crashes in the Amazon or the Andes and the survivors pull themselves, scratched and bleeding, out of the smoking, bent aluminum and suddenly face Raw Nature? Remember how gradually the ones with the "right stuff" came forward? These were the ones who refused to give up. The ones who quickly learned to make do with what was at hand and were wise enough to quickly forget about the way things used to be. They rose to the occasion. And surprise of surprises. Some of them turned out to be fat, little spinster maidens and nerdic-looking short guys who wore thick glasses, the kind of guys who years ago Charles Atlas promised to reshape so that big, muscle-bound beach bums would not get away with kicking sand in their eyes. Well, Hollywood was for a nanosecond striking a chord of reality that has great psychological relevance for all of us would-be catastrophe survivors. The more usual Hollywood dreamland fantasies, which often titillated us with the possibility that we, too, might own a penthouse and drive a Mercedes Benz or Bently, don't seem to have much relevance when the ground is shaking drastically beneath our feet, water is inundating our home or heavy airborne particulate matter is now choking off our breath. Ah, those wonderful stereotypes we've been trained on, programmed by, bought with. Those deadly, lying stereotypes. They have come to dominate too much too many people's existence. To threaten it. Especially in times of great stress when we must be capable of giving ourselves an instantaneous and honest reality-check.

We must rearrange our thinking before it is too late and we are caught off guard. Be certain that no matter how much you plan for disasters, even great, catastrophic earth changes, they will come like a ghost in the night and you will be startled, shaken by their suddenness and lurid, noisy demeanor. Unless you have prepared your mind, and truly wish to survive, you probably will not. You may instead shatter like fine glass or go raving off into the dark night never to be heard from again.

A good mind must come to realize the preciousness of life, all life--or that mind, and the body that houses it, will soon perish. The life force is the great mystery which gives us being, consciousness and, most probably, meaning. No one has seen, as far as I know, the face of God or whatever Creative Force is the initiator and maintainer of conscious reality. But there are enough hints around that this Creative Force does truly exist. Perhaps intuition is as good an indicator as any. Many people have suggested, and I among them, that pure logic iself should lead us gradually to the idea of a Great Initiator, even without the extant "scientific" indications that an intelligent, ordering, controlling force does in fact exist in the cosmos. As Albert Einstein put it, "God does not play dice" with creation. It may well be that each of us through experiential living--above and beyond any religious programming or formal education--must learn this to his or her own satisfaction. Then soul-peace is possible. Then this various and often confusing concatenation of events we call life begins to make sense. Then we begin to understand how everything is intimately interrelated to everything else, sometimes in what seem the most intriguing, marvellous ways. Everything is nexus and plexus with everything else, and thus the idea of the Oneness of creation is born. I, for one, cannot believe that whatever would create us as a part of Itself does not love us. It is natural to love that which issues forth from yourself, if you are mentally healthy.

I offer here the potential earth-change survivor an argument. It is an argument for the preciousness of your life, including a proposition to keep on going as long as you can in this body in this world until you can go on no longer. At that point, I would say you have reached your natural end. At that point *que sera, sera.* What will be, will be.

The argument I offer you is not the only one possible. There are, as you well know, innumerable arguments, a multitude of philosophies, that bid for your attention in this world. But I think we need ask more often than we do, Which argument holds the Creative Force most precious? A great many philosophies--which are no more than extended arguments--make grand postures, reek of subtle conceptions, only to break down and smell bad when the essential question is asked, "But how precious is life in this argument?"

Once the natural end occurs through accident, disease, old age, earth changes or some other agent, then we can say the play has been played, the last act rung in, the curtain calls (if, indeed, there has been time for any) all made. The actor has finished his role, entertained and instructed those who are within his purview and learned (hopefully) from their responses. This is, I believe, the way it was intended to be. Each of us precious living beings are here for a time to experience, to learn and to grow mentally and spiritually as much as we can. There is a proper time for everything, as our ancient Judeo-Christian scriptures so well indicate, "For everything there is a season, and a time for every matter under heaven: a time to be born, and a time to die . . . ." The actors, the play, the last act. Then new stages, new plays *ad infinitum* on a cosmic scale few of us have really contemplated and barely understand. Encouragingly, if we can believe our greatest prophets (and I do), the actors gradually become wiser, more loving, more tolerant, the plays perceptibly less violent as we approach a perfection in our being that reflects a far greater Perfection that overshadows us and guides us. At first this guidance is almost imperceptible to us, but as time goes on we learn to see more and more clearly, beyond the fog that is the heritage of our lower nature.

There are some other facets to my argument. You need not accept them. They are not quite as inspirational as what has preceded. I doubt that they are as crucial to the greater scheme of things as is an appreciation for the preciousness of the Life Force. But they are tangentially relevant and I find them interesting, so I will give them to you for your inspection. They concern primarily the perspective we have on our bodies while in this life and also the propagation of multiple bodies (what I am going to call "containers" for mind and spirit) over time. We should subsume these topics under the designation of reincarnational ideas where they most properly belong.

I have already indicated how we humans are deluged with our own propaganda. One of the chief focuses of that propaganda, which we manufacture at such a furious rate to justify ourselves in all our confusion, is the idea of the physical body as supreme, the "body spectacular" proposition. It has a corollary which goes like this, This body is the only body you'll ever get, so you better go for the gusto--and the devil take the hindmost. At the same time as we are "enjoying" these ideas (which inevitably leave us sad and empty, because our logical mind tells us this beautiful body is gradually wearing out), we give lip service to mercenary ecclesiastics, most of whom do not really believe their own utterances. These utterances at their best, however, backed by scriptures, suggest that it is the spirit of man which endures and is primary; that the body is but a passing thing.

And passing it surely is. In spite of advertising trumpets which proclaim its virtual immortality. In spite of modern science which frenetically searches for ways to extend its longevity. In spite of all the will power (and makeup) countless humans expend trying to slow (or hide) its natural, degenerative course. Despite its perishability, we need not in all honesty be ashamed of it, once we admit its limitations. But certainly it is the height of idiocy to overglorify it, as is our popular custom today. One does not have to be an inveterate conspiratorialist to be aware that there are powerful and wealthy people (unmitigated materialists) who thrive because of such thinking.

We can quickly become slaves to the dead-end philosophy that we only have one body and one life. And enslaved by the people who preach and teach such philosophy. Or we can escape to a brighter one which makes our brief tenure on this planet this time around much more meaningful, a philosophy which in fact has much evidence supporting it. I will address the ramifications of it in a moment. In fact, I am eager to do so.

First, however, let's talk a little more about the human body--that physical mass of energy that is the container for our mind and spirit whose presence, and overall reality, causes us so much confusion so much of the time. It is amazing how many people are ashamed of their bodies and what bodies do. A little ashamed or a lot ashamed--depending upon the man or woman. What is the cause of this psychological malady? Basically a mind that has become confused by false religious influences and popular ideas about what the body really is. These popular ideas, not surprisingly, are advocated quite often by the popular media, which sometimes through ignorance and sometimes malevolently and selfishly pass them on to the public, which is caught up in a quiet psychological tug of war between feelings of hedonistic delight and a guilty conscience.

The philosophy you are being offered here is an alternative way of thinking, a more natural one. In it the body is not portrayed as an adversarial, repugnant thing, neither does it stand as "number one" in priority. It is simply recognized as a mass of solidified energy, as is this world, both being so for particular reasons. The main reason for the body being as it is, as I have already suggested, is as a vehicle to house mind and spirit so that they may experience, learn and grow in a particular ambience--this world. A world, by the way, among many worlds, one house among many mansions. Not the best of houses, granted, but not the worst either. And relatively speaking, not the "highest" and not the "lowest." But a particular kind of world, special in its own way and certainly in many locales breathtakingly beautiful, singing at its peculiar, one-of-a-kind pitch, resonating at its unique frequency. This pitch and frequency are matched to you. That is why you are here.

You say that sounds like New Age philosophy and you're suspicious? Call it what you like. A toad by any other name is still a toad, a princess still a princess. What I have proposed is nothing some of the ancients of this world did not know. And the wisest of them learned how to accommodate themselves to this world. Gautama

Buddha realized the mind must be controlled by will power--if the mind was not to be continually assaulted by the various illusory demons it is capable of manufacturing in plentiful supply. The Great Nazarene concluded that the way of accommodation was to "overcome" the limitations of earth-living. Overcome them and you change your frequency. Then this world is no longer matched to you. You are ready to remove yourself elsewhere where you are a better fit.

What is most important is to realize that the would-be earth-change survivor would do well to hold fast to this life as long as possible, then let what will be be. That is what this book is all about--overcoming, surviving, guarding the precious life force in the form of the body as long as possible, until the natural end, whenever that may come, however that may be. We must not give up the life force within the container until the proper moment of time. And the way we accomplish this is to remember Gautama's great lesson and use mental firmness, our will power, to overcome our adversity. The life force of the spirit is indestructible, that of the mind probably so, if we are to believe our greatest sages, and I see no reason why we should not. While we are in body, let us appreciate it, without shame, with joy, sharing it lovingly, respectfully and carefully with others if we wish. And if we are wise, I think we will avoid buying into the dead-end game of the "body spectacular" which is a kind of low-level debauchery backed by a shortsighted philosophy that posits "That's all there is." One of its premises is that maximum consumption to feed the body is one of the highest ideals to be attained in earth life. This is a kind of vampirism if you stop to think about it, a literal ingestion of more solidified energy than the "container" needs to operate efficiently. About the best thing you can say about this kind of display is that it is preferable to the type of vampirism which feeds off of other people's mental and spiritual energy . Regrettably, the two kinds are often found together. A thinking human being should not want to be enslaved by such limited perspectives or behavior.

I have been speaking of "natural ends" which are imposed by the natural course of the life force. In contradistinction to natural ends would be artificially-induced ends. It is no secret that in this confused world of ours there is an increasing rate of suicide, especially among young people. If our teachers and preachers were more in tune with the currents of the cosmic life force, they would have a more sustaining philosophy of life to offer confused humanity. Unfortunately, most of them are just as confused as their students and congregations. No wonder so many turn away in disgust and despair. As the traditional values and sustaining customs of Western life have crumbled, nothing equally sustaining has been offered to the masses and certainly nothing potentially better. The world still lacks, as always, a loving *modus vivendi.* But now it finds itself bereft of even the rudiments of a considerate civility. And the great psychological truism, which is a continuing bane to us all, rises up always like a fiendish gargoyle looking now more frightful than ever: Until human beings learn to love and respect themselves better, there is little hope they will show much love and respect to their neighbors.

Mental firmness, or will power, like many of the other mental and spiritual characteristics of mankind, is at least in part learned behavior. Some of us have learned sooner and better than others. Quite probably some of us have been around eons longer than others, which is one more good reason not to judge others. We simply don't know enough (about them and things in general) to dare to do so.

There are, it would seem, various kinds of mental firmness. Some kinds wear better than other kinds. Some are intended for the long haul, some for the short. Here is an example of one kind. I mention it because it happened recently and is fresh in my mind.

I was deep-sea fishing off the coast of Puerto Vallarta, Mexico, with a companion fate had turned my way. He was not a young man although he did not qualify quite yet as an old man of the sea. We introduced ourselves, shook hands and soon got down to business.

Business that day was sailfish, marlin and dorado. We had been skimming our baits for some time without success when we had a "take." My new friend was quickly into a large sailfish which went majestically crashing and skipping the wave tops, alternately to make deep, powerful, underwater runs. The battle had been joined and it promised to be a memorable one.

On fairly light tackle a ten-and-a-half-foot Pacific sailfish is a powerful adversary. A sailfish of such size foul-hooked in the side of the head, as this one turned out to be, makes fighting and landing such a beauty doubly difficult. Let me say now that we had agreed from the beginning to release all billfish caught. This was a sporting concession which, in this day and age of depleted stocks, has strong arguments in its support. Fate, however, had different plans.

The Mexican sportsfisherman my new friend and I had chartered did not have a permanently mounted fighting chair. There were instead two heavy, plastic chairs each with a gimbel in which to insert the rod end when the going got rough. These chairs, lacking a solid base, had a disturbing tendency to dance around the deck. And the chair-gimbels were not strong. Result: My friend broke both gimbels and was soon left with a bare rod, no fighting belt, and only his lower stomach to cushion the fish's pressure as his chair went scooting disconcertingly out of control.

It was a long, long battle. I watched my friend's face change over time from ecstasy to agony. Sweat poured from his face and body in great rivulets. The temperature was in the 90's, the humidity close to 100 percent as is normal for Novembers in that part of the subtropical world. My friend was suffering. I could see that plainly. And yet, by the rules of the game, I could do nothing for him.

This was a determined man. That much soon became obvious. He was hurting but holding firm. Little did I know then as the minutes passed how tempted he was to give it all up. I only understood later, when he told me some of the thoughts which swarmed in his mind like captured angry bees looking for a release.

He said there were moments when he almost cried out and said "Enough of this" and passed the rod to me. He said he thought he must be crazy to let himself get beat up like that. I remember him falling to the deck several times thumping hard his knees and legs. Later he told me his lower stomach was a mass of deep bruises.

"I almost quit," he said. "Several times. But I just couldn't say the words. Why in hell should a fish be so important? I kept asking myself. But I wanted to finish what I had started. I thought it was important to do so. Although if you would have asked me at the time, I would have been hard pressed to give you reasons why. I still think it was important to finish it. I'm glad I did. I wanted desperately to finish what I had started if at all possible."

And he did finish what he had started. I could see that. The captain and first mate were impressed. I, being somewhat a neophyte at saltwater big-game fishing, was awed and my respect for my new friend soared.

We had to keep this fish because, not only was it badly torn by the hook in the side of its head, but it was thoroughly spent and probably, in the mind of the captain, could not recover. We took the captain's word for that and decided to bring the fish in, to be cut and divided among the poor. There are many poor people who flock to the docks in such cities and villages. It was good to know that the meat would not be wasted.

The battle between the fish and my new friend was a draw. Those were his own words. It took him, he said, a full week to recover physically from his experience. "I don't regret it," he hold me. "I feel I'm a better person for what happened. I only wish the brave fish could have lived. He deserved to do so."

Why do I tell you such a story when far greater problems seem to exist in the world calling out for attention and care? For this reason. The story is an example of a kind of mental firmness that is more easily captured and framed than other, more complicated or extended kinds. Call it short-term mental firmness if you like. A person sets a definite goal, makes up his mind to do a certain thing, and then proceeds, despite sometimes great difficulties, to reach that goal. I call it the Edmund Hillary-Mt. Everest syndrome. If the goal is positive, the experience is productive. If the goal is selfish and mean, the world is no more the better, and we can count ourselves lucky that the scale of most of these negative endeavors is small. It is, significantly, this kind of short-term, goal-oriented mental firmness, this kind of persistence, which may make it possible for the earth-change survivor to overcome the initial shocks of severe earth changes. Human will power should never be underestimated. Mental firmness requires a will that may bend but refuses to break.

There is a longer term mental firmness that we all must master if we are to withstand for extended periods of time the slings and arrows of outrageous fortune, including a time when all natural balances seem awry and nature itself (including, perhaps, human nature) appears to have turned against us. I call it the Alexandr Solzhenitsyn--*gulag* syndrome, but one brief story cannot comprehend its bounds or do justice to the multitudinous variety of types and variations of this kind of mental firmness. Suffice it to say it does not give up over the long haul. The survivor battles on sometimes against ridiculous odds with the expenditure of much sweat, many tears and very real blood refusing to release his vision (and life force) until he has no choice. At its worst, it is nothing but pure stubbornness and objectively has little to recommend it. At best, it humbles the human ability to give it a worthy description. It has been demonstrated by Jewish prisoners of the Holocaust, by partisan volunteers tortured by the Nazi and other fascist and inhumane governments even to this day, by the victims and survivors of the Soviet *gulags* of a few years ago and many other brave people the world over in a yesterday of yesterdays. This kind of long-term mental firmness, under the most trying conditions, often in the most vicious of circumstances, has helped insure the survival of the human race. As William Faulkner so aptly

155

voiced in his Noble Prize for Literature acceptance speech, there is something special in man that advocates most beautifully for his continuing endurance in this whirling, havoc-prone, most difficult of worlds.

14

Keeping the Spirit Uplifted

A man who is poor of spirit is hardly a man at all. But a man rich in spirit is much more than a mind or the sum of his bodily parts. He is a survivor no matter the conditions--an evergrowing, evermore sparkling reflection of the Life Force which gave him original being, sustains him, and continually creates multifarious realities and synergistic connections in a variety of frames of reference around him.

What the final cosmic reality may be, whether it is a merging of partial reflection and greater reflector or something else altogether, I cannot say. But woe to him who misses that pregnant moment in relativistic time, that meeting-moment of he who would understand with that which knows and understands and seems to have, from the cosmic hints we have been able to garner, compassion for the truly curious soul. To be totally uninterested in learning all we can about ourselves and creation, to care less or not at all about the possibility of seeing the last moment through--if indeed there is a last revelatory moment--is to be soul-dead. I can think of nothing more terrible or more demeaning to the life force within us than such an attitude.

We must never submit to spiritual vegetation. To do so is in direct contradiction to spiritual evolution just as not valuing the body as long as life force breathes within it is contrary to physical evolution. The wise man knows that both evolutions issue from the same father and are nourished by the same mother. And it is interesting to observe that, at least in this dimension of reality, physical evolvement and enlightenment are, for all practical purposes, proportionately related.

To paraphrase Einstein once again, there seems to be few, if any, accidental rolls of the dice in creation. If this is true, then whatever happens to this planet, and this solar system and galaxy, is not fortuitous but has its own logic and meaning. This likewise applies to us, you and me, because we are a part of it all. We may not understand the full import of what encompasses us all about but its meaning awaits our discovery. It is not inconceivable that it yearns for us to do so that it may better commune with us. It is also not inconceivable that we have either chosen to be here now or else we have been assigned here for a special reason: so that we might learn to commune better under these particular conditions at this specific moment in time. Whatever the case, we are here and find ourselves called to action. And we have a great choice to make, whether to act or not.

Thus we find ourselves faced with a great mystery and a mighty paradox. Neither is new. Philosophers have tussled with both throughout recorded time without being able to draw incontrovertible conclusions. The great mystery concerns the nature of creation and our place within it. There is a general uncertainty as to what the creation is. Will we ever have a better understanding of it and our place within it? Several decades ago the celebrated English physicist and novelist C.P. Snow, surveying the animosity that had developed between science and art, each with its preferential ideas as to the best method to understand and explore reality, became convinced of the necessity of closing the gap. "When those two senses have grown apart, then no society is going to be able to think with wisdom." If the alert spirit of man is to remain uplifted, it would seem advantageous for it to forsake little and to use any and all methodologies, as long as they are compassionate, to help it explore further the nature of creation and our particular relationship to it.

The great paradox that faces us concerns free will or lack of it. Are we really free spirits? Should we bother to act willfully or not? Does it really matter? Has the record already been cut and we are just grooves waiting for the needle to scratch us and set us to singing or moaning? If we can, will we ever have a better understanding of the creation and our place in it? Why not let the cataclysms roll over us? What's the use?

We have, as far as our science and art have been able to discern, and to agree, the gift of at least a partial free will capable of interacting with this creation. Under the circumstances, our best course might well be to accept the idea of partial free will (until we find out for certain it is an illusion), accept personal responsibility for our actions, and hope that by meeting our challenges we will gain greater insight into realities which at this time we do not very well understand. Thus the mystery remains veiled. But we can make a great assumption, a leap of faith, perhaps, but one backed by some good, empiric evidence and some telling, intuitive experience. We can assume that the human spirit, growing apace over time like a well-suckled child, is becoming all the while more capable of communion. By choosing to do nothing, by not acting willfully, it is pretty well guaranteed that we will learn little spiritually or otherwise. We simply won't grow very much. And we will have forfeited our chances for a greater communion.

If earth changes are in our future, then we had best prepare ourselves to face them, to act and react as is necessary. We will undoubtedly learn much about ourselves and our relationships to those around us in the process. We may well discover a multitude of things to be related in ways we never suspected.

We may learn, for example, sometime in the not-too-distant future, that our former thoughts and actions have created, or helped create, the world we now know--and even that our present thoughts are directly influencing the kind of changes that we are now experiencing and will experience in the near future. If we are aware that everything is intimately related to everything else, everything affects, influences, everything else, these revelations will come as no surprise to us. Here we have room for the idea of an active free will and the demonstration of its efficacy. I can foresee the day in the not too distant future when a neoteric science will dedicate itself to the exploration of this greater synergy and the effects of free will applied to it.

Once we accept the idea that everything affects

everything else, we can better understand some of the many possibilities inherent within complex interactions. Things which seem out of our control may not, in fact, be so very different from those things which we seem to have some control over--such as our daily thoughts and actions. It is not ridiculous to speculate that simultaneously occurring evolutionary phenomena of a system, such as is taking place right now in this solar system, on this planet and within, for that matter, each freewill-exercising human being, are not mutually exclusive. We simply do not have a proper appreciation for the breadth and scope of the greater cosmic ecosystem. When a shoe drops on earth, it does send reverberations (however tiny) throughout the solar system and beyond--whether there is a human ear to hear them or not. We must make every effort to get away from the kind of fallacious philosophical thinking that demands a human presence for reality to exist, the kind of anthropocentric and ethnocentric perspectives that still plague our sciences and our arts.

Each human being "makes waves" all the time. Each spirit residing in a body is either positively or negatively affecting creation every moment of its existence. How powerful these waves are in each instance and each instant is relativistic. What is important is that a "wave" is sent out and our impact is somewhere, sometime registered. Often the impact is almost immediate and the site of the impact is another human being. It would be very dangerous and foolish of us to ever minimize in our minds the effects of a human being's influence on this world or the heavens.

Each human being, simply by being alive and active, is important in the greater scheme of things. This is not always obvious. The media today quietly militates against such thinking. Yet even in this century, where earthly governments and organized religion have helped foster the notion that the individual is of minimal importance and influence, the individual soul can take comfort in its cosmic position. It is definitely a wave-maker, either of one magnitude or another, but a wave-maker nonetheless. Because we are here, we are automatically a responsible integer in the earth's equation whether we want to be or not. Our influence in that equation does not depend ultimately on governments or churches but greatly on the quality of the spirit which imbues us.

We choose what kind of "waves" we make. A happy, well-adjusted spirit tends to make positive ones. A positive attitude radiating positive waves during the many crises of massive earth changes will help lighten the psychological stress others are feeling.* A negative attitude can be counted on to depress other survivors. God only knows how our negative waves penetrate into creation and what effects they have. Hopefully, the Creator catches them somewhere in center field like a Lenny Dykstra and buries them in a cosmic black hole somewhere out of harm's way.

It would be well for catastrophic earth-change survivors to never forget that, no matter how demanding their experiences, the spirit and mind are registering and recording everything. What the spirit records and how the mind chooses to respond to experience are crucial to the evolutionary progress of the individual. It is easy to forget this during momentary stress. The physical body in duress does not like to be bothered with abstract and seemingly

---

*The popularity of Norman Vincent Peale's *The Power of Positive Thinking*, and similar books, should not surprise us. Positive thinking is the master key to soul growth as well as happy living.

162

useless ideas. The mind is tempted to become short-sighted and self-serving, the body brutish in its reactions. The spiritual part of man, unless called upon and made to serve and direct, can easily be shut out. Selfless sacrifice, the desire to aid and share, tolerance and respect for others can rapidly disappear. The history (and prehistory) of mankind seems to indicate that during periods of massive earth changes, society most often degenerates into brutishness. Every individual, every community of survivors, must make a continuing effort to remind itself that the individual and collective mind and spirit are in danger of rapid degeneration and terminal rot unless great pains are taken to maintain the finest qualities of both.

It would be a good idea for members of any survival community to meet periodically, perhaps weekly, to review their responses and actions to the challenges they must meet. Only the highest standards are acceptable. Anything less will gradually undermine the humanity of the community. This may sound idealistic. It is not. There are two tracks leading to barbarity. One is sudden and fairly mindless (e.g. Idi Amin's track). The other is slow and filled with rationalizations (e.g. Stalin's and Hitler's track). The former tract is very often taken by either an individual who finds himself in absolute, unchallenged control (as in Amin's case) or by the human being who suddenly finds himself removed from all former, familiar and supportive restraints. A good inclusive example of the former track is Joseph Conrad's character Kurtz, who discovered the true heart of darkness was not Africa but his own heart, which had turned to savagery.*

*The reference is to Joseph Conrad's novel, *Heart of Darkness*.

History suggests the latter track has been the way of innumerable civilizations which, having decided to take the "practical approach" to governing and living and to give only lip-service allegiance to natural cosmic morality, slide inexorably into decline. Sometimes the slippage is quite gradual, like the Roman Empire's, or not so gradual, as happened with Nazi Germany. The result is, however, virtually the same: a state where the highest qualities of mind and spirit are little valued or cease to be valued at all. Such we now see happening in Armenia and Azerbaijan, in Somalia, in Liberia, Iran, Iraq, within the separated states of the former Yugoslavia, in the Ukraine, Crimea, Georgia and perhaps Russia itself as well as in many other places in the world.

If savagery can so easily become the lot of nations untested by massive earth calamities, imagine what is possible when *all* civil organizations that are capable of maintaining a semblance of order are no longer functioning.

Many good minds have despaired of writing and speaking about uplifting the human spirit and keeping it uplifted. This line of thought, according to one variation, presupposes that only those who have achieved a certain level of enlightenment are capable of the necessary understanding to profit spiritually from further instruction. A corollary idea seems to be that this type of enlightened individual, after exploring for a time his own "inner space," will naturally seek later in "outer space" what is most congenial with his newly discovered inner vision. Perhaps this explains why Gautama and the Great Nazarene did not for the most part actively recruit disciples but instead let them naturally gravitate toward them. The Nazarene's parables, for example, were definitely not meant for the masses. They could not understand them, as he well knew. Interestingly enough, most of his disciples could not either.

Ancient, great sages taught orally. Pythagoras and Socrates, among others, surrounded themselves with bright, young men eager to explore new ideas. It was these students who put styli to parchment, who became the scribes of their masters. Ideas were floated in the air, and those who thought they could catch them were welcome to try.

Today's Zen masters seldom speak. Words are recognized as an extremely faulty system of transmitting truth. It is better to be silent than a jabberwocky of an external reality which is filled with paradoxes. Either one knows or doesn't know. Until one does know, the teacher is practically useless. But the student of life must learn from personal experience what it is about. Such enlightenment cannot really be taught. Ironically, once the student does "know," the teacher is thoroughly useless.

Western tradition has not supported very well the idea of the "inner space" quest with one outstanding exception- -certain practices of the Amerindians, particularly the "vision quest." Life is seen as revolving almost solely around exterior reality. The practical man addresses himself to practical things. The opposite type of personality is labelled a "dreamer" and the connotations are all pejorative.

This Western mindset has placed disastrous limitations on the parameters of our understanding. We have become outward-looking men only who give little shrift to the dazzling and various worlds of mind and spirit. If we were more willing to become inward-oriented at least part of the time, we might discover rich and wondrous realities which far exceed that to which we have become accustomed and which so often seems to bore us with its predictability. We might also discover that these inner realities will lead us more quickly to enlightenment than a monomaniacal fascination with "outer space." Our science today does not believe this. Our educational systems do not teach it.

Recent Western history has produced few acknowledged and respected proponents of the value of the inward-quest philosophy. The William Blakes, Emanuel Swedenborgs, Helen Blavatskys and their like appear to stand out more as philosophical oddities than representatives of mainstream Western thinking. It is worthy of note, however, that within the last 20 years a small but growing, loose but peaceful, army of adherents to the inner-way philosophy has become increasingly visible in Europe and the Americas. Somewhat predictably, it has attracted imitative camp followers and, at this point, it is often difficult to recognize the serious practitioners from their playacting counterparts.

How much individual and societal damage has been caused by our philosophical myopias is hard to tell. My guess would be that it is vast though mostly uncharted. I think it is safe to conclude, however, that a man or woman who is operating physically, mentally and spiritually almost totally in the outer world frame of reference, and neglecting an exploration of inner space, is functioning at a great disadvantage. He/she is like a perfectly healthy swimmer who insists on using only one arm and one leg. If you asked him why he swims as he does, he would say it is because he has always done it that way. If this swimmer is too stubborn or too benighted, for whatever reason, to discover his wholeness and what that wholeness is capable of accomplishing, he will never find out how far and how fast he might have come.

I still believe in the efficacy of words, spoken or written, even with all their limitations. I believe in sound and will choose it over silence when I am convinced it can precipitate change for the better. And I am enough of a true Westerner to believe in the efficacy of three dimensional experience, a true empiricist as long as the empiricism is balanced with, and invigorated by, a thorough searching out of inner space. I have learned inner space and outer reality are not mutually exclusive. Together they form creation as it is to be found on this plane of existence. It is a creation at once numbing and exhilarating in its seemingly infinite possibilities. We would do well to learn as much as we can from both realities and are denying ourselves much if we ignore either or give an overwhelmingly disproportionate amount of our attention to one or the other.

I do not believe, however, that our two realities are quite equal in educational potential. I favor the greater utilization of inner space for several specific reasons. First, inner space exploration has distinct advantages. It opens windows to other dimensions, offers multiple planes of being, whereas three dimensional reality leaves us landlocked (earth bound) and a victim of our senses only. Secondly, the greatest advantage of exploring inwardly is that it can lead us more quickly to greater understanding whether that understanding be personal or cosmic. It is not only the quickest route but the most objective. This is exactly opposite of what we have been taught. Thirdly, everything to be found in outer reality can be found in inner space. Although we may find outer reality entertaining and helpful, we must finally come to admit, I believe, that it is inevitably comprehended by, and really only an adjunct of, inner space.

Within inner space, we can explore energy and matter in all its variations. Outer space limits us to the exploration of energy frozen at certain frequencies. Why mistake the elephant's tail for the whole creature (creation)? Partially blind leaders of men who are totally committed to outer reality--and this includes most of our advertising executives, media tycoons, politicians, educators and the majority of our contemporary philosophers--can only lead us to flawed, partial truths. They are playing without realizing that a fuller deck exists. The cynic might add that it is obvious many politicians start out with less than a full deck and play accordingly throughout their careers. The reference, of course, has little to do with cosmology, cosmography and theories of reality. But let's not miss the main point. Any philosophy which hopes to have a chance of adequately circumscribing and defining what man is and what constitutes reality (even reality as we experience it on this plane) must address both inner and outer space simultaneously or it will fail as all have done up to now.

Any science which hopes to be reflective of the greater reality cannot ignore the inner nature of man or it also will fail. And any society which hopes to be whole and harmonious, at once healthy and happy, cannot support, even unconsciously, a dichotomy of science and the arts, as C. P. Snow long ago recognized. The dichotomy that now exists reflects a perverse failure to observe accurately and transcribe adequately the intimate interrelatedness of all energy and matter (including human relations) in their various forms of manifestation.

These considerations may seem academic, moot questions to individuals caught up and seemingly trapped by the demands of massive earth changes. These individuals might well ask, "What in the world does this have to do with us, we who have to struggle so hard for shelter over our heads and a few scraps of food?" I can understand that kind of response. But consider further for a moment. Isn't it quite possible that even the most naturally burdened man or woman who is mentally strong and spiritually in balance could be at the same time in harmony with the greater total reality? Even the most primitive Aborigine? Does that seem absurd? I don't think so.

Certainly the plain, simple lifestyle of present-day Mennonites, Amish and traditional Hopi indicates to us that a reasonably good life can be lived without many of the creature comforts associated with contemporary living. If I am correct, this kind of practitioner of the art of simple living has increased his/her chances of physical survival greatly during cataclysmic periods. I think most people would agree that a man or woman who is physically, mentally and spiritually in harmony with themselves has a better chance of surviving crises, no matter what their nature or number, than someone who fancies himself at the cutting edge of what is civilized and is overburdened with the complexities of that civilization. If this is true, we had best rearrange our thinking in regard to the harmonious primitive man's potential for attainment, spiritual and otherwise.

There is another way of conceptualizing harmony in relation to the greater, total reality. It is as follows:

Let us consider ourselves as quantums of energy. Each of us is composed of a combination of quantums of energy. They are in contact and communicate to one extent or another. Each person's quantums are also in contact with the quantums of others--also with the non-human quantums which surround us and make our reality, earthly, solar and cosmic.

The quantum of energy within us that is most primal and primary is our spiritual essence. This is timeless, does not seem to change and is in direct contact with Primal Creative Force. It is actually the same stuff, a chip off the old block. Each individual quantum carries within it the blueprint and the potential capacities of the Larger Chip from which it came, although its abilities to create and make changes are somewhat lesser in degree than the Larger Chip itself. This description is, as you may well recognize, a form of the traditional Cosmic Father/Son or Cosmic Mother/Progeny paradigm that orthodox religions have so diligently expropriated and so marvelously misunderstood and misused.

The quantum of energy that is the spirit has always been (or seems so) and will always be (or seems so). It is indestructible. No earth change can destroy it. No nuclear holocaust obliterate it. No gunshot wound from a confused mugger in a distraught city can take it away from you. It is essential you--forever.

Working together with this Spirit quantum is a Soul/Mind quantum. This is also you in all your eternal personality guises. It is everything that you have ever learned in this life or in others. It is the unique aggregate of experience and understanding that no one else anywhere has, not exactly anyway. The energetic Spiritual quantum inhabits, permeates, the energetic Soul/Mind quantum. But the Soul/Mind quantum is often confused and forgetful. It is even more confused and more forgetful the less it is working in harmony with the Spirit quantum. Sometimes it even forgets there is a Spirit quantum present. This is the state of affairs of a good part of humanity at the moment and, for that matter, has always been.

The Soul/Mind quantum is carried from one life to the next, from one world, one plane, one dimension to the next. It is usually only in contact with the given plane on which it is residing at the time, although this need not be so. Remember that. It is crucial to the present argument. The Spirit quantum, however, is always in touch with all planes, all dimensions, all worlds simultaneously. The Soul/Mind quantum is not, unfortunately, usually aware of this fact.

The Body quantum is a container made from the elements of this world. Without the Soul/Mind quantum and Spirit quantum to guide it, imbue it with intelligence and purpose and give it cosmic consciousness, it is at best an animal, at worst no more alive than the atoms of more solified energy that make up other animal forms and even less animate forms such as plants and even rocks. It is best to remember, however, that the simplest atoms wherever found, whether singular or in combination, are "alive." The question for us is how alive, as measured by consciousness and intelligence, and finally, how much in conscious communication with the greater cosmic consciousness that pervades all beingness?

The "goal" of all energy forms, including matter, whether it is conscious or not, seems to be a greater, more thorough communication with this greater cosmic consciousness. Each mass of energy would know Each until All knows All. The goal is total communion (or, as some theologians would say, a return to total

171

communion).

Let's recapitulate for the sake of clarity. For the immediate moment we find that, in this world, our Spirit quantum and Soul/Mind quantum have decided to house themselves for practical reasons in a material Body quantum. Think of the body, as I have indicated, as little more than a container. It is useful and serves its purpose for a time rather well, which is to supply a material vehicle to get around in and explore this material world, which is nothing more than energy transmogrified to a certain number of frequencies.

I think you can see what I'm getting at. We are explorers. We are here to learn. Our goal is greater communion not only with things in and of this world but with everything everywhere. I do not want to get into arguments about whether the Soul/Mind quantum is always immortal and everlasting. It seems to be, although it may not be. Perhaps it can be destroyed or taken back, subsumed and consumed by the Greater Creative Force. I don't know. We all know, however, from our experience that the Body quantum is very vulnerable. It lives for a few decades, ages and dies naturally. Or by accident. Or disease. Or abuse. It is not a vehicle in which to trust very much or in which to put much "faith." Or to worship, as so many people, particularly younger ones, are wont to do. But as a practical container to hold the Spirit and Soul/Mind quantums in this world as they go about their business, it is serviceable enough. It will do.

What "business" am I talking about? Ideally, if all quantums are working perfectly in harmony, we would have a situation that could be described as follows. The Soul/Mind quantum is aware of the Spirit quantum and its great powers. Therefore the Soul/Mind quantum would frequently (or continuously) meld with the Spirit quantum, *thus putting it in continuous contact with all of creation, all being.* The Soul/Mind quantum would not restrict itself unknowingly, as it most often does now, to contact with this world and this world only. Because to do so often gives false images of what the greater creation is all about. Too many of us are drawing conclusions from insufficient evidence, a logic teacher might say. *Because our Spirit quantum touches everything and inherently knows all, there is no reason why we should ever be lonely or feel abandoned in a hostile or indifferent universe.* The greater creation is anything but innately hostile and never truly indifferent, although the Soul/Mind quantum with its self-imposed limitations creates the illusion of such.

There is no need why our Soul/Mind quantum and Spirit quantum should ever suffer and despair. It is true that we may lose our Body quantum at any moment due to unforeseen circumstances, but this is not an occasion for depression. When a "container" wears out or is lost, a new container is always available if that is what the Soul/Mind quantum truly desires. Friends are not lost. The Spirit quantum is always in contact with them and all other manifestations of spirit everywhere. We suffer needlessly from the delusions of a "lower" world caused by the failure of our Soul/Mind quantum to rise above the *seeming limitations* of this kind of matter/frequency/energy.

Granted, "seeing" clearly in this world is difficult. It could be likened to a swimmer who dives below the water's surface and then tries to make out shapes and sounds originating from above the water's surface. The picture is blurry, the sounds greatly muffled and distorted. He can, however, with practice know that reality above

173

him better. But depending exclusively or primarily upon the senses of his Body quantum will not do it. They fail here. Their great limitations become obvious. If our metaphorical swimmer in this world wishes to "see" more than his physical senses can provide for him, see more of this world or plane and dimensions beyond, he had best finally harmonize as much as possible Spirit, Soul/Mind and Body quantums. Then he will be better able to "see" *here and there.* He would be well advised, however, to value and protect his Body quantum as a useful vehicle for as long as he can--not give it up too soon or too willingly. It is, after all, the proper functional vehicle for a certain kind of exploration. Everything, as the saying goes, has its own time. This reasoning applies even if we realize that against the backdrop of the greater cosmic picture, time is an extremely relative conception.

I can think of no better way to close this discussion than to quote a remark made by C. G. Jung, "When Lao-Tzu says: 'All are clear, I alone am clouded,' he is expressing what I now feel in advanced old age." I could not more heartily agree, although I am yet in middle years. And I am tempted to blame the clouds on an imperfect harmony of Spirit, Soul/Mind and Body quantums within myself. But I am apt to forgive myself until I can do better, because there is something in me that intuits cosmic harmony and is thoroughly convinced of its existence. I have seen the hints of it in this world and will follow them as best I can. They make me want to dance and plant my garden.

Let the elements rage and the great earth changes come if they must. I realize that all things change in order to evolve and I with them. Like the delicate butterflies of my garden, those ancient symbols of immortality, I will give up the breath of this life when the proper time comes. And not a moment sooner. I will give it up, die and fly off with my singular allotment of energy into other adventures elsewhere.

Sometimes, in a luxurious moment of leisure, I stretch back and gaze with wonder at my simple garden. I have noted with care and some pleasure over the seasons that the corn dies that it may grow again, and in that process and promise I find a great satisfaction.

Retrospect

Our situation analysis indicated an acceleration of major earth-change events since the late 1980s. These events--such as the weather-affecting eruption of Mount Pinatubo in the Philippines, major hurricanes Andrew and Hugo, severe earthquakes in Armenia, Nicaragua, Iran, southern India and the Los Angeles area (USA), to name only a few examples among many--are not only becoming more frequent but, in many cases, more pronounced in magnitude. The upsurge of damaging typhoons and tropical storms, such as those which have whipped the coasts of Mexico, Japan and other parts of Asia, are further evidence that earth-change activity is on the upswing, as is the recent record flooding in the United States, Europe and Asia.

Recent studies of glaciers in the Andes and Alps have indicated that a global warming trend is indeed a fact. Global temperature changes of only a degree or two can be predictably counted upon to cause vast weather changes in the planet's near future. Whether this global warming trend is a precursor of a new major Ice Age down the road or only an intermediate phase between major Ice Ages is uncertain. Whatever the case, present inhabitants of planet Earth would appear to have enough to worry about now and in the immediate, foreseeable future.

It would appear likely that astrophysicists and astronomers have greatly underestimated the possibility of an extraterrestrial object, such as a large comet, meteor or asteroid, impacting the earth. For example, we have twice witnessed since 1989 the "near miss" of the large asteroid Toutatis and have had several close calls with other asteroids. One explanation for the scientific community's ultraconservative attitudes and estimates probably lies with its subservience to the Lyellian theory of "uniformitarian" change, a theory which, upon close inspection, is riddled by much conventionally acceptable geologic evidence as well as by a host of impressive disconformities, erratica and anomalies, all of which suggest that planet Earth has undergone numerous and extensive catastrophic periods, many of which affected either all of the planet or significantly large portions of it. Oxygen 18 (O^{18}) ice core samples from Greenland and Antarctica suggest many periods of major climatic alteration, even short-cycle, periodic changes, although glaciologists generally speaking have been slow to look for short-cycle evidence of such changes or to recognize it when they see it. Mindsets prevail here as much as they do in formal, academic geology, geophysics, astronomy and astrophysics.

It has not been the intention of this work to cry wolf and foment fear within a population which is already gravely fearful and suffering the effects of a civilization almost totally bereft of its traditional (and formerly sustaining) value systems. But the fact remains that most people are totally unprepared for the consequences of large-scale earth changes; witness the suffering and confusion caused by the flooding in 1993 in the Mississippi river valley and in Florida (1992) during and after hurricane Andrew. Both of these earth-change events, although restricted in area *and not nearly as devastating as cataclysms striking other parts of the world around the same time*, demonstrated how ill-prepared (though undoubtedly well-intentioned) are our emergency relief organizations, whether they are private, federal or state-controlled in nature. It does not take much imagination to realize that a multiple number of these "minor" natural alterations occurring simultaneously would totally overburden the capacity of government to deal with them. What reaction then might we expect from an asteroid impact which affected the whole world at once?

It is our conclusion that it is the individual who must prepare himself/herself to survive such calamity. Those who trust in others to do so for them are being either unthoughtful, lazy or foolhardy.

Our intention was to offer a very basic, practical guide, a book that could be read on the run and, if remembered, could make the crucial difference between survival or not. The facts of survival have been placed in a social context, which is where they properly belong, and the added commentary which accompanies matters of fact is intended to explore the social implications of cataclysmic events. The upsurge of earth-change events as we near the turn of the century is, as far as the author is concerned, totally coincidental. He in no way subscribes to end-of-the-century, catastrophe theories which, as folk superstitions go, have a long, painful tradition. He does recognize, however, that the present earth-change activity seems to parallel and support certain biblical and nonbiblical prophecies.

This is not a work for the weekend survivalist who enjoys pushing himself to extremes. And it is not intended as a "secret code" for combative types who hope that by accumulating enough ammunition and foodstuffs, they will be certain to insure their own survival and, shortly thereafter, the erection of a political state more to their liking. It is intended, for everyone, especially for all those well- meaning-at-heart urbanites and suburbanites who recognize the potential of massive earth changes and who are, at the moment, totally unprepared to deal with such a reality but would like to learn how.

One does not have to be a genius to survive--nor just lucky. There are steps that can be taken to greatly increase the odds of survival, steps involving the accumulation of: emergency foodstuffs, long-term food supplies, basic tools, basic clothing and inexpensive respiration devices. It is possible as well to learn to construct basic emergency shelter and to take other actions of a lifesaving nature.

Inevitably as important as these down-to-earth considerations are, there are equally important questions of community formation, defense and education of adults and the young. It has been our intention to offer ideas, some relatively new and admittedly theoretical, some older and more proven.

The last two chapters are by far the most abstract and philosophical ones to be found in this work. They are also without a doubt, in the author's opinion, the two most important ones. The first of these discusses mental firmness as a characteristic not only worth cultivating in its own right but as a necessary prerequisite for the individual who finds himself, perhaps for the first time in his life, stretched and stressed beyond limits he thought he could not endure. The larger truth is that there are few, if any, limits beyond which the serious, trained mind, in conjunction with a harmonious spirit, cannot go.

The last chapter discusses the unique spirit of man and the necessity to make every effort during all our waking hours, in times of stress and in times of joy, to recognize its special energy and to make sure, as much as possible, that our mind-energy and body-energy are in harmonious contact with it. We have suggested that the Spirit quantum of man is in touch with all of creation all of the time. We believe few people are aware of this or the fact that their minds are the link between the actions of the body and the spirit. The mind is the great facilitator, the great expediter, but without direction from the Spirit quantum, it knows neither what to facilitate nor how to go compassionately and most effectively to work.

Only when these three quantums of energy (Spirit, Mind, Body) are balanced and working properly together can the individual, on this plane or elsewhere, whether extremely stressed or at rest, maximize his potential for survival and growth. Whether we are at work for something so mundane as the survival of the body or busying ourselves with something so grand as an attempt to more accurately understand the larger cosmos, we will continue to be exposed to the great forces which drive creation and which seem, sometimes with the greatest care and sometimes willy-nilly, to move us about or send us reeling.

Literature Cited

Albritton, Claude C. *Catastrophic Episodes in Earth History*. London: Chapman, 1989.

Alvarez, L. W. "Mass extinctions caused by large bolide impacts." *Physics Today* 40 (1987): 24-33.

Alvarez, W., and R. A. Muller. "Evidence from crater ages for periodic impacts on the earth." *Nature* 308 (1984): 718-20.

American Geophysical Union. *Greenland Ice Core*. Washington: AGU, 1985.

Austin, S. A. *Catastrophes in Earth History*. El Cajon: Creation Research, 1984.

Axelrod, D. I. "Role of volcanism in climate and evolution." *Geological Society of America Special Paper* 185 (1981): 1-59.

Back to Basics. Pleasantville: Reader's Digest, 1981.

Bellamy, H. Schindler. *Built before the Flood: The Problem of the Tiahuanacu Ruins*. London: Faber, 1943.

Berggren, W. A., and John A. Van Couvering, eds. *Catastrophes and Earth History*. Princeton: Princeton UP,1984.

Blong, R. J. *Volcanic Hazards*. Sidney: Academic Press, 1984.

Brooks, C. E. P. *Climate Through the Ages*. London: Benn, 1926.

Brown, Hugh Auchincloss. *Cataclysms of the Earth*. New York: Twayne, 1967.

Bryant, Page. *The Earth Changes Survival Handbook*.

Santa Fe: Sun, 1983.

Buckland, W. *Reliquiae Diluvianae: or Observations on the Organic Remains Contained in Caves, Fissures, and Diluvial Gravel, and on Other Geological Phenomena Attending the Action of a Universal Deluge.* London: John Murray, 1823.

Cannon, Dolores. *Conversations with Nostradamus.* Rev. ed. Vol. 2. Huntsville: Ozark Mountain Publishers, 1992. 3 vols.

Carter, Mary Ellen. *Edgar Cayce on Prophecy.* New York: Paperback Library, 1968.

Chaij, Fernando. *Preparation for the Final Crisis.* Mountain View: Pacific, 1966.

Cheetham, Erika. *The Prophecies of Nostradamus.* New York: Putnam's, 1975.

Clark, D. H., W. H. McCrea, and F. R. Stephenson. "Frequency of nearby supernovae and climatic and biological catastrophes." *Nature* 265 (1977): 318-19.

Close, Frank. *End.* London: Simon, 1988.

Clube, V., and W. M. Napier. *The Cosmic Serpent.* New York: Universe, 1982.

Cohane, John Philip. *Paradox: The Case for the Extraterrestrial Origin of Man.* New York: Crown, 1977.

Donnelly, Ignatius. *Atlantis.* New York: Gramercy, 1949.

- - -. *Ragnarok.* New York: University Books, 1970.

Flint, R. F. *Glacial Geology and the Pleistocene Epoch.* New York: Wiley; London: Chapman, 1947.

Ganapathy, R. "Evidence for a major meteorite impact on the Earth 34 million years ago: implications on the origin of North American tektites and Eocene extinction." *Geological implications of impacts of large asteroids and comets on the Earth*. Ed. L. T. Silver and P. H. Schultz. Boulder: Geological Society of America, 1982. 513-16.

- - -. "A major meteorite impact on the Earth 65 million years ago." *Science* 209 (1980): 921-23.

Gibbons, Euell. *Stalking the Blue-Eyed Scallop*. New York: David McKay, 1970.

- - -. *Stalking the Wild Asparagus*. New York: David McKay, 1962.

Goodman, Jeffrey. *We Are the Earthquake Generation*. New York: Berkley, 1982.

Hooykas, R. *Catastrophism in Geology*. Amsterdam: North-Holland, 1970.

Howorth, Henry H. *The Mammoth and the Flood*. London: Sampson Low, 1887.

Illustrated Guide to Gardening. London: Reader's Digest, 1975.

Jochmans, J. R. *Rolling Thunder, The Coming Earth Changes*. Santa Fe: Sun, 1980.

Kavasch, Barrie. *Native Harvests*. New York: Vintage-Random, 1979.

Kirkwood, Byron. *Survival Guide for the New Millennium*. Nevada City: Blue Dolphin, 1993.

Lambert, W. G., and A. R. Millard. *Atra-Hasis, the Babylonian Story of the Flood*. Oxford: Clarendon, 1970.

Lamont, Andri. *Nostradamus Sees All*. Philadelphia: Foulsham, 1944.

Leoni, Edgar. *Nostradamus and His Prophecies*. New York: Bell, 1982.

Lyell, C. *Principles of Geology*. 3 vols. London: John

Murray, 1830-1833.

Muck, Otto. *The Secret of Atlantis*. New York: Pocket, 1979.

Muller, Richard. *Nemesis*. New York: Weidenfeld and Nicolson, 1988.

Nelson, Ralph, trans. *Popul Vuh*. Boston: Houghton, 1976.

Peake, Harold. *The Flood*. New York: Robert M. McBride, 1930.

Preston, E. W. *The Earth and its Cycles*. London: Theosophical Publishing House, 1931.

Prestwich, Joseph. *On Certain Phenomena Belonging to the Close of the Last Geological Period and on Their Bearing upon the Traditions of the Flood*. London: Macmillan, 1895.

Price, George McCready. *Evolutionary Geology and New Catastrophism*. Mountain View: Pacific, 1926.

Rampino, M. R., and R. B. Stothers. "Terrestrial mass extinctions, cometary impacts and the Sun's motion perpendicular to the galactic plane." *Nature* 308 (1984): 709-12.

Raup, D. M. "Biological extinction in world history." *Science* 231 (1986): 1528-33.

- - -. *The Nemesis Affair*. New York: Norton, 1986.

Raup, D. M., and J. J. Seploski. "Mass extinctions in marine fossil record." *Science* 215 (1982): 1501-03.

- - -. "Periodic extinctions of families and genera." *Science* 231 (1986): 833-36.

"Safety woes still linger after quake." *Milwaukee Sentinel* 21 Jan. 1994: A3.

Schellhorn, G. Cope. *Extraterrestrials in Biblical Prophecy*. Madison: Horus House, 1990.

- - -. *When Men Are Gods*. Madison: Horus House, 1991.

Seasons of Changes, Ways of Response. Virginia Beach: Heritage, 1974.

Shoemaker, E. M. "Asteroid and comet bombardment of the Earth." *Earth Planet. Sci., Ann. Rev.* 11 (1983): 461-94.

Shoemaker, E. M., et al. "Earth-crossing asteroids: orbital classes, collision rates with earth, and origin." *Asteroids*. Ed. T. Gehrels. Tucson: U of Arizona P, 1979. 253-282.

Silver, L. T., and P. H. Schultz, eds. *Geological Implications of Impacts of Large Asteroids and Comets on the Earth*. Proc. of a conference on large body impacts and terrestrial evolution. 19-22 Oct. 1981. Boulder: Geological Society of America, 1982.

Sitchin, Zecharia. *The 12th Planet*. New York: Avon, 1978.

Stothers, R. B. "The great Tambora eruption of 1815 and its aftermath." *Science* 224 (1984): 1191-98.

Taylor, Alfred E., ed. and trans. *Timaeus and Critias*. London: Methuen, 1929.

Toon, O. B. "Sudden changes in atmospheric composition and climate." *Patterns of Change in Earth Evolution*. Ed. H. D. Holland and A. F. Trendall. Berlin: Springer, 1984. 41-61.

Turco, R. P., et al. "Tungushka meteor fall of 1908: effects on stratospheric ozone." *Science* 214 (1981): 19-23.

U. S. Army Survival Manual. New York: Dorset, 1992.

United States. FBI. *Uniform Crime Reports for the United States, 1991*. Washington: GPO, 1992.

- - -. - - -. *Uniform Crime Reports for the United States, 1992.* Washington: GPO, 1993.

Velikovsky, Immanuel. *Ages in Chaos.* New York: Doubleday, 1952.

- - -. *Earth in Upheaval.* New York: Pocket, 1977.

- - -. *Worlds in Collision.* New York: Delta-Dell, 1965.

Warshofsky, Fred. *Doomsday.* New York: Reader's Digest, 1977.

Waters, Frank. *The Book of the Hopi.* New York: Ballantine, 1963.

Webre, Alfred L., and Phillip H. Liss. *The Age of Cataclysm.* New York: Berkley, 1974.

Wegener, Alfred L. *The Origin of Continents and Oceans.* New York: Dutton, 1924.

West, Cornel. "The '80s: Market Culture Run Amok." *Newsweek* 3 Jan. 1994: 48-49.

Wetherill, G. W. "Apollo Objects." *Scientific American* 240.3 (1979): 54-65.

Whewell, W. Rev. of *Principles of Geology,* by C. Lyell. *Quarterly Review* 93 (1832): 103-32.

White, John. *Pole Shift.* Virginia Beach: A.R.E., 1986.

Whitmire, D. P., and A. A. Jackson. "Are periodic mass extinctions driven by a distant solar companion?" *Nature* 308 (1984): 713-15.

Whitmire, D. P. and J. J. Matese. "Periodic comet showers and Planet X." *Nature* 313 (1985): 36-38.

Williamson, George Hunt. *Road in the Sky.* London: Neville Spearman, 1959.

Zabel, Morton Dauwen, ed. *The Portable Conrad.* New York: Viking, 1947.

Index

Abercrombie 54
Abrahamsen, Aaron 4
accidents, cosmic 31
Ackerman, Thomas P. 38, 71
advertising 142
Afganistan 9
Africa 10, 20, 76, 163
Africa, Horn of 94
Agassiz, Louis 16
Ages in Chaos (Velikovsky) 16
Alabama 106
Alaska 68, 122
Albritton, Claude 137
Alexandria, library of 133
Algeria 11, 67
allergies 114
Alphonso the Wise 12
Alps 176
Alvarez, Luis 72, 136
Alvarez, Walter 136
Amazon 143
America, North 10, 18, 124
Americans, native 122
Americas 166
Amerindians 121, 165
Amin, Idi 163
Amish 46-47, 169
Anderson, Doc 4
Andes 143, 176
Andrew, hurricane 12, 176, 178
angelos 19
anomalies 136, 177
Antarctic 25, 177
anunnaki 63

Apocalypse, Four Horsemen of 32, 128
Apocalypse Now 78
Arabia 134
Arctic 25
Aristarchus 134
Aristophanes 133
Arizona 24
Arkansas 24
Armageddon 76, 101, 128, 134
Armenia 11, 164, 176
Army surplus 69
Arnold, Matthew 75
Asia 10, 176
asteroids 14, 177
astroblemes 135
Atlanti, Shawn 128
Atlantis 22, 138
Atlas, Charles 144
Audubon Society 103
Axelrod, D.I. 67
axis, shifts of 3, 13, 20-22, 25, 38, 56-57, 101, 136
Azerbaijan 164

Baalbek 135
Babbitt 75
Babylonians 13
Bali 68
Bangladesh 9, 94
Banyacya, Thomas 18, 119
bartering 86
BCCI (Bank of Credit and Commerce International) 127

190

particulate matter 25, 68-72
Patten, Donald 136
Peale, Norman Vincent 162
Pennsylvania 10
Pepperdine University 129
Peru 9, 25
Petra 135
Phaeton 57
Philippines 9-10, 176
philosophy, New Age 149
philosophy, Western 166
photosynthesis 94
Pinatubo, Mount 9-10, 68, 176
pit garden 95-96
Planet of the Apes 79
plants, open-pollinated 98-100
Plato 57-58, 137
poisoning, mushroom 113-16
Pollack, James B. 38, 71
Polonius 106
Pompeii 69
Popocatepetle 9
Power of Positive Thinking
(Peale) 162
Prestwich, Joseph 16, 136
Price, George McCready 16,
136
primitivism 138
prophecies 4, 19, 21, 178
prophecies, Hindu 4
prophecies, Hopi 18
prophecies, Incan 4
prophecies, Judeo-Christian
4, 178
prophecies, Mayan 4, 18
prophet(s) 19
prophets, self-proclaimed 101
Pro-tech, Inc. 70
proverb(s) 35, 80-81, 131

psychics 4
Puerto Rico 14
Puerto Vallarta 50, 152
puffer fish 121
Punjab 8
Pythagoras 165

radioactivity 38
Raup, David 136
Red Cross 49
Renaissance 126-27
respirators 69-72
Revelation, Book of 13, 15, 38
rice 48
Ring of Fire 9-10, 25, 68
Rio de Janeiro 125
Rio Grande river 50
Rivera, Amaury 4, 13
Roberts, Jane 24
Roman Empire 126, 164
Rome 126, 134
rotation, axis 3
Russia 94, 164

SAC (Strategic Air Command) 37
Sacsahuaman 135
safe areas 8, 28
Sagan, Carl 38, 71
Sahel 94
Saint Helens, Mount 68
Sais, priests of 137-38
salt 49
Salvation Army 49
Samothrace 134
San Blas 122
San Francisco 11, 22, 25
sanitation 50
Scallion, Gordon-Michael 4
science, academic 135

Toon, Brian 38, 71-72
tornadoes 10
total man 27-28
Toutatis 14-15, 177
toxins, fish 121
Trismegistus, Hermes 134
Trueblood, Ted 62
tsunami 9, 25
TTAPS report 72
Turco, Richard 38, 71
Turkey 9, 11
typhoons 176

UFO(s) 18-19
Ukraine 164
Uniform Crime Report (1992)
124
uniformitarianism 1-3, 135, 177
uniformitarianism, punctuated 3
United States 50, 112, 176
United States, central 30
United States, northeastern 10,
22, 68, 143
United States, northern 112
United States, Rocky Mountains
24
United States, southeastern 22
United States, southwestern
24, 37
United States, western 37
United States, western coast 22
Unzen, Mount 10
U. S. Geologic Survey 50
U. S. Safety, Inc. 70
Utnapishtum 26

Valerio, Joao 4
values, social 126, 177
vegetables 95-98

vegetarians 117
Velikovsky, Immanuel 16, 136
Vesuvius 69
Victory Gardens 45
Vietnam War 78
Virginia 21-22
Virginia Beach 21-22
vision quest 165
Volcanic Hazards (Blong) 66
volcanism 9, 11, 25, 66-71

Wagner, Richard 71
Walden 74
Walden, or Life in the Woods
(Thoreau) 74
Wallace, Baird 4
Wal-Mart 55
Walton, Isaak 122
war, nuclear 38
Washington 68
water, drinking 50-53, 64
water, fresh 50-51
weather, "freak" 10
Wells, Sixto Jose Paz 4, 14
Werner, Abraham Gottlob 136
West, Cornel 125
West, far 108
West coast 22
West Virginia 10
Western World 126, 133, 142
Wetherill, G.W. 15, 136
When Men Are Gods (Schellhorn)
5, 126
Whewell, William 16, 136
White Sulphur Springs 37
White Sulphur Springs Hotel 36
Whitmire, Daniel 136
wild West 87
will to live 34

Books Available from HORUS HOUSE PRESS

True Account of ETs Contacting Government Engineer
THE WHITE SANDS INCIDENT
Dr. Daniel W. Fry
$10.95

The Bible and Ancient Astronauts
EXTRATERRESTRIALS IN BIBLICAL PROPHECY
G. Cope Schellhorn
$12.95

The Hunt for Ancient Atlantean Records
DISCOVERING THE LOST PYRAMID
G. Cope Schellhorn
$8.95

ET Sign Language and Earth Change Essays
A MESSAGE FROM THE STARS
Mary M. Wunder
$11.95

How and Why Man Becomes the Ultimate Cosmic Quester
WHEN MEN ARE GODS
G. Cope Schellhorn
$12.95

How Loch Ness Dragons and UFO Serpents Intertwine
SERPENTS OF THE SKY, DRAGONS OF THE EARTH
F. W. Holiday
$13.95

Horus House Press, Inc., P.O. Box 55185, Madison, Wisconsin 53705-8985
Please send me the book(s) I have checked above. I am enclosing
$_____. Please add $1.50 for postage and handling for each
book ordered. WI residents must add 5% sales tax. No CODs or credit
cards please. Canadian & foreign customers add $2.00. Please allow
4 to 6 weeks for delivery.

Name _____

Address _____

City _____ State _____ Zip code _____